Writing Skills

Grade 4

Flash Kids

Flash Kids
A Division of Barnes & Noble
122 Fifth Avenue
New York, NY 10011

Dear Parent,

Reading and writing well are essential tools for success in all school subjects. In addition, many states now include writing assessments in their standardized tests. There may be no precise formula for good writing, but through studying samples and practicing different styles, your child will build the skills and versatility to approach any writing assignment with ease and confidence.

Each of the six units in this fun, colorful workbook focuses on a unique type of writing that your fourth-grader may be required to use in school or may wish to pursue in his or her free time. These types include personal narrative, how-to writing, fable, comparative writing, descriptive writing, and short report. The first half of each unit reinforces writing aspects such as putting ideas in a sequence, using descriptive details, working with a thesaurus, and using proofreading marks, in addition to providing fun, inspirational writing ideas for your child to explore alone or with a friend. The second half of each unit focuses on a practice paper that exemplifies the writing type. After your child reads the practice paper, he or she will analyze it, prepare a writing plan for his or her own paper, write a first draft, revise it, and, lastly, allow you or a friend to score it.

Here are some helpful suggestions for getting the most out of this workbook:

- Provide a quiet place to work.
- Go over the directions together.
- Encourage your child to do his or her best.
- Check each activity when it is complete.
- Review your child's work together, noting good work as well as points for improvement.

As your child completes the units, help him or her maintain a positive attitude about writing. Provide writing opportunities such as a journal, in which your child can write about things that happen each day and can keep a running list of topics or story ideas for future writing projects. Read your child's stories aloud at bedtime, and display his or her writing in your home.

Most importantly, enjoy this time you spend together. Your child's writing skills will improve even more with your dedication and support!

Proofreading Marks

Use the following symbols to help make proofreading faster.

MARK	MEANING	EXAMPLE
⬯	spell correctly	I ⟨liek⟩ dogs. *like*
⊙	add period	They are my favorite kind of pet⊙
⋏	add comma	I also like cats⋏ birds, and bunnies.
?	add question mark	What kind of pet do you have ?
≡	capitalize	My dog's name is scooter. ≡
/	make lowercase	He has ⫽rown spots.
ℒ	take out	He likes to ~~to~~ run and play.
∧	add	He even likes to get ∧ bath. *a*
∿	switch	Afterward he ⁄all⧵ shakes⟩ over.
¶	indent paragraph	¶ I love my dog, Scooter. He is the best pet I have ever had. Every morning he wakes me with a bark. Every night he sleeps with me.
˅ ˅	add quotation marks	˅You are my best friend,˅ I tell him.

4

Table of Contents

UNIT 1
Personal Narrative
6-26

UNIT 2
How-to Writing
27-46

UNIT 3
Fable
47-66

UNIT 4
Comparative Writing
67-88

UNIT 5
Descriptive Writing
89-106

UNIT 6
Short Report
107-124

Answer Key
125-128

UNIT 1: Personal Narrative

HOW MUCH DO YOU KNOW?

Read the paragraph. Then answer the questions.

My great-uncle Daniel had his seventy-fifth birthday last week. He told us an amazing story at his birthday party.

Daniel's Grandpa Weaver had made bricks many years ago. Daniel and his family were not very interested in bricks. Everyone forgot about Grandpa Weaver's old brick business.

Uncle Daniel and his brothers grew up and moved away. All of them married and had children of their own. Daniel and his wife were schoolteachers for 40 years.

Uncle Daniel and Aunt Ginny built a brick patio in their backyard last summer. Some friends told Uncle Daniel about a place to buy bricks. He and Aunt Ginny drove several miles to look at the bricks. All the bricks lay in a pile near an old house. Uncle Daniel bought several of the bricks. He and Aunt Ginny looked at the bricks in amazement. The name "Weaver" was stamped on them. The bricks had been made by my great-great-grandfather more than 150 years ago!

1. What does the narrative reveal about the writer's great-uncle?

Daniel's Grandpa Wevile Made
bricks many years ago

2. What details did the writer use to describe Uncle Daniel and Aunt Ginny?

Uncle Dainel is seventy five, They were
school teachers for forty years.

3. What happens at the end of the narrative?

They went to by some
bicks and found out that they were
made by Darnael's gandpa.

Analyzing a Personal Narrative

A PERSONAL NARRATIVE

- is written in the first person
- describes an experience important to the writer
- gives details about the experience in time order
- reveals the feelings of the people who took part

Read the narrative. Then answer the questions.

In third grade I never cared much about bicycles. An old two-wheeler with thick tires was fine with me for all the riding I did.

A few days before my tenth birthday, Dad took me shopping. I wanted a skateboard, but he steered me to the bike department. It was there that I saw the beautiful bike. It was a racing bike with pink tires.

I sat on the seat, and it was just my size. I was delighted! To my surprise, Dad wasn't pleased at all. He looked at the price tag and shook his head. "Maybe they'll put it on sale sometime, Sue," he said as we walked away.

On my birthday Dad brought in a huge box. I lifted the lid, and inside was the best surprise I'd ever had: the bike! Dad and I both had tears in our eyes as I hugged him.

1. What do you learn about the writer at the beginning of the narrative?
   She didn't care much about bicycles in third grade

2. What does the narrative reveal about the writer's father?
   he likes suprises

3. What happens at the end of the narrative?
   She gets the bike she wanted.

4. How do the writer and her father feel about each other?

They were happy with echother and were so happy they cried.

Visualizing Events and Recalling Feelings

> **TO CREATE PERSONAL NARRATIVES, GOOD WRITERS**
> - picture events and remember feelings before beginning to write
> - write about events and feelings in an order that makes sense

Read the story. Then answer the questions.

Carlos is sure that if he lives to be a hundred, he will never forget his little sister's eighth birthday. She had opened her presents from Mom and Dad and Grandma, and she was starting to dress her new doll. Then Carlos said, "Wait, Cristina, look!" He handed her the box he had hidden under the table, the box with the gift he had saved for weeks to buy.

The room grew quiet as everyone gathered around. Cristina's eyes were shining with excitement. "Listen!" she whispered. Tiny scratching noises came from the box.

"Open it, Cristina!" Grandma said, smiling.

With trembling fingers, Cristina lifted the lid. "Oh, Carlos! Oh, Carlos!" was all she could say as she snuggled the tiny black kitten to her cheek. Seeing her joy, Carlos thought he had never been so happy.

1. Which details did the writer use to describe things Carlos saw?

She was sorting to dress
her new doll. Crisinas
eys were shining with exsitment

2. Which details did the writer use to describe things Carlos heard?

"Oh, carlos" "Oh, carlos"

3. Which detail did the writer use to tell how Carlos felt?

Carlos had never been so Happy.

Using Vivid Words

Good writers use vivid words to describe people's feelings.

Rewrite each sentence. Add vivid words or replace dull words with livelier ones.

1. Last summer my family had a nice vacation.

   Last summer in July my family had a great vacation!

2. The first part of the trip was not good.

   The first hour was very bad while we drove.

3. It was a 1,000-mile drive.

   It was a long long 1,000 mile drive to Colorado Springs.

4. I was glad when we finally arrived in Colorado Springs.

   I was relieved when we finaly arived in colorado springs.

5. One day we took a nice ride to the top of Pikes Peak.

   One day we took a great ride to the very top of Pikes Peak.

6. The view from the top of the mountain was pretty.

   The view from the top of Pikes Peak was spectacular.

7. Some small chipmunks took peanuts from our hands.

   10 cute tiny chipmunks ate penuts out of our hands

Using the Thesaurus

> Good writers use a thesaurus to find vivid and exact words.

A. For each sentence, replace the word in parentheses ( ) with a more vivid or exact word from a thesaurus. Be sure the new word makes sense in the sentence.

1. Jared is _____ an excellent
   (really)
   football player.

2. The other players on his team don't think he is

   _____ just because he is deaf.
   (different)

3. It was _____ for Jared to find a team that would accept
   (hard)
   a deaf player.

4. Now Coach Taylor is _____ that Jared is playing for
   (happy)
   the Pioneers.

B. Use a thesaurus to find an antonym, or opposite, of each word. Then write a sentence using the antonym.

5. sad _____

   _____

6. cheer _____

   _____

7. tiresome _____

   _____

Proofreading a Personal Narrative

Proofread the beginning of the personal narrative, paying special attention to spelling. Use the Proofreading Marks to correct at least six errors.

PROOFREADING MARKS	
◯	spell correctly
⊙	add period
⋏	add comma
?	add question mark
≡	capitalize
/	make lowercase
⟋	take out
⋀	add
∿	switch
¶	indent paragraph
ⱽ ⱽ	add quotation marks

See the chart on page 4 to learn how to use these marks.

Who could ever fourget the terrible

sandstorm we had last march? It was one of

the most frighetning experiences of my life!

For many months there had been

almost no rain. December, Janurary, and

February had been especially dry. No rain

fell in March, either, but the wind began to

blow furiously. On many days the sky was more brown than blew because the air was so filled with sand. The sand even crept inside hour house. Every morning my bed felt gritty. As I walked to and from school, blowing sand stung my ears, eyes, and cheeks

One afternoon was expecially scary. We all looked anxiously through the classroom windows as the sky grew darker and darker. Our teacher, Mrs. Robertson, tried to tell us a storry, but no one could listen. The wind howled, and we felt sand settle on our desks. Suddenly, everything was as dark as midnite. The electricity had gone off!

Write a Personal Narrative

Write a story about a shark from the shark's point of view. Tell how it feels to be a shark. Be sure to give details about the experience in time order.

_____
_____
_____
_____
_____
_____
_____
_____
_____
_____

Write a Journal Entry

With a friend, make a list of qualities it takes to be a friend.

_____   _____

_____   _____

_____   _____

Use your list to write a journal entry about what it means to be a friend. Give details. Be sure to reveal your feelings. After you have revised and proofread your journal entry, read it aloud to your friend.

_____

_____

_____

_____

_____

Write about an Important Event

Remember, when you write a personal narrative, you are expressing your feelings about an experience that is important to you.

Remember an important event, such as a recent birthday or your first day of school. List details from that day.

_____   _____

_____   _____

_____   _____

_____   _____

Write a personal narrative about that important event. Include the details in your story.

_____

_____

_____

_____

_____

_____

_____

_____

(Continue on your own paper.)

Write a Travel Story

With a friend, discuss places you have traveled in your state or city. Tell about interesting things you did or saw. Choose one place. Write a story telling about your travels. Be sure to give details about the experience in time order.

Yay we are finely going snow skiing. It's an 8 hour drive from Tulsa to breachen ridge. When we got their it was to aly to check into our hotel room. While we were wating to check in we rented skis and ski boots for me, miriam, and Samuel, Mom and Dad. It was finely time for ski school. we went over to the gractes course. Our teacher taught us how to turn and how to stop. After Lurch I got to go on the montin. we stopt to get hot choclate. then we skied on the blues and the greens.

A Practice Personal Narrative

A FRIEND AT THE RIGHT TIME

I love to tell the story about how I met my best friend. My best friend's name is Tiger. We met at the school fair.

At first, my friend's name surprised me. But I guess it shouldn't have. After all, my name is Sunny. People who know me often wonder how I got that name.

Each year, all the fourth-grade classes hold a school fair. Everyone in fourth grade works at the fair. Some kids get to work inside the booths. Others take care of the little kids who ride the rides. Unfortunately, I got the second job. I don't really like taking care of little kids. My brother is a little kid, and he drives me crazy. But there was one good thing about the job. That's where I met Tiger.

At first, my job at the fair didn't seem so bad. I helped little kids get on the back of a pony. The pony was beautiful and gentle. It didn't seem to mind all those kids half as much as I did. I got tired of telling them to wait their turn. I got tired of hearing them cry for their parents. But more than anything, I got tired of holding their ice cream cones while they rode around. One thing was clear to me. There are problems that come with being older and more responsible.

The day wasn't even half over, and I was already splattered with ice cream. I looked like I had the measles, but the chocolate, vanilla, and strawberry kind. Suddenly, a little boy came screaming into the pony ring. "Oh," I thought, "not another screamer."

The boy grabbed the pony's reins. The pony stopped, and the kid on the pony's back started to fall. The little boy was falling away from me. His eyes were big and filled with tears. He was falling fast.

I stretched over the pony to reach the boy. At the same time, I saw a flash of fur go by my legs.

Tiger grabbed the pony's reins and pulled the pony away from my legs. I caught the boy seconds before we both hit the ground. The boy sat on top of me. He was laughing at the ice cream smeared on my face. "Very funny," I thought to myself. I got up and rubbed my backside. Maybe next time I'll just let the kid fall.

I looked for the pony. It was just a few feet away. Its reins were in Tiger's mouth. Thanks to Tiger's fast action, I saved the little boy. We were both heroes. And Tiger, the fastest dog I've ever known, was my new best friend.

Respond to the Practice Paper

Write your answers to the following questions or directions.

1. What clue tells you why the writer wrote this story? In other words, what is the writer's purpose for writing?

   _____

   _____

2. What is the setting for this story? In other words, where does it happen?

   _____

   _____

3. What did you learn about Sunny from reading this story?

   _____

   _____

4. Write a paragraph to summarize this story. Use these questions to help you write your summary:
   - Who is the story about?
   - What are the main ideas in the story?
   - How does the story end?

   _____

   _____

   _____

   _____

   _____

   _____

   _____

Analyze the Practice Paper

Read "A Friend at the Right Time" again. As you read, think about how the writer achieved her purpose for writing. Write your answers to the following questions.

1. How does the writer let you know that this story is a personal narrative?

   _____

   _____

2. In the sixth paragraph, the writer tells the story's problem. What is it?

   _____

   _____

3. What did the writer do to solve her problem?

   _____

   _____

4. What is the purpose of a conclusion in a story?

   _____

   _____

5. How are the first paragraph and the last paragraph in this story alike?

   _____

   _____

Writing Assignment

As people grow and change, they may have many best friends. Think about the best friend in your life now. Think about writing a personal narrative that tells about your best friend. Use examples and details to show why this person is your best friend. Use this writing plan to help you write a first draft on the next page.

Name your friend:

▼

Tell how you and your friend became friends.

▼

Give examples to show why this person is your <u>best</u> friend.

First Draft

TIPS FOR WRITING A PERSONAL NARRATIVE:

- Write from your point of view. Use the words *I, me*, and *my* to show your readers that this is your story.

- Think about what you want to tell your reader.

- Organize your ideas into a beginning, middle, and end.

- Write an interesting introduction that "grabs" your readers.

- Write an ending for your story. Write it from your point of view.

Use your writing plan as a guide as you write your first draft of a personal narrative. Include a catchy title.

_____

_____

_____

_____

_____

_____

_____

_____

(Continue on your own paper.)

Revise the Draft

Use the chart below to help you revise your draft. Check YES or NO to answer each question in the chart. If you answer NO, make notes to remind yourself how you can revise, or change, your writing to improve it.

Question	YES ✔	NO ✔	If the answer is NO, what will you do to improve your writing?
Does your story tell about your best friend?			
Do you start your story by introducing your friend?			
Do you describe events in the order they happened?			
Does your conclusion summarize your story in a new way?			
Do you make it clear why this person is your best friend?			
Do you use words such as *I*, *me*, and *my* to tell your story?			
Do you explain how you feel about your best friend?			
Do you include important details?			
Have you corrected mistakes in spelling, grammar, and punctuation?			

Use the notes in your chart and your writing plan to revise your draft.

Writing Report Card

Read your revised draft again or ask someone else to read it. Have the person who reads your paper complete the following Report Card. Revise your paper until you have no less than a Very Good Score for each item.

Title of paper: _____

Purpose of paper: _*This is a personal narrative.*_____

Person who scores the paper: _____

Score	Writing Goals
	Does this story tell about something that happened to the writer?
	Does the story have a good beginning, or introduction?
	Are the story's main ideas organized into paragraphs?
	Are there enough details to support each main idea?
	Are the paragraphs organized in a way that makes sense?
	Are there different kinds of sentences that help make the story interesting?
	Does the story have an ending?
	Are the story's grammar, spelling, and punctuation correct?

☺ Excellent Score   ☆ Very Good Score   + Good Score
✔ Acceptable Score   − Needs Improvement

UNIT 2: How-to Writing

HOW MUCH DO YOU KNOW?

Read the paragraph. Rewrite it, putting the steps in the correct order.
Then answer the questions.

Homemade peanut butter is easy to make. Spread on bread or crackers and eat! Next, put peanuts in a blender. First, shell the peanuts. Blend them until they are smooth. Last, stir in a little cooking oil and salt.

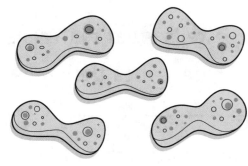

_____

_____

_____

_____

_____

_____

_____

1. What is the topic sentence of the paragraph?

    _____

    _____

2. What information does the last sentence give?

    _____

    _____

Analyzing a How-to Paragraph

A HOW-TO PARAGRAPH

- has a topic sentence that tells what the audience will learn to do
- tells what materials are needed
- describes the steps in order

Read the paragraph. Then answer the questions.

"Musical Chairs" is a good game to play with a group of friends. You will need some chairs and a radio or stereo. One person should be in charge of starting and stopping the music. First, count the players and subtract one. Then place that number of chairs in a circle facing outward. Next, the players walk around the circle of chairs as the music plays. When the music stops, each player tries to sit in a chair. The one who is left standing is out of the game. Then, remove one chair from the circle and continue the game. When only one chair is left, the player who gets it wins the game.

1. What is the topic sentence of the paragraph?

   "musical chairs" is a good game to play with friends

2. What information does the topic sentence give?

   _____

3. What information does the first detail sentence give?

   _____

4. What information do the detail sentences in the middle of the paragraph give?

_____

5. What information does the last sentence give?

_____

Visualizing Steps in a Process

WHEN WRITING A HOW-TO PARAGRAPH, GOOD WRITERS

- make a movie in their heads of the steps in the process
- write directions for the steps in the order in which they happen

Read the steps to make a kite. Then complete the paragraph.

1. Trace the outline of the kite onto a sheet of plastic.
2. Cut out the kite.
3. Glue the frame to the back of the kite.
4. Add a tail and decorations.
5. Attach the kite string.

To make a kite, first _____

Then _____

Next _____

Then _____

The last step is to _____

Writing for an Audience and a Purpose

GOOD WRITERS HELP A READER UNDERSTAND DIRECTIONS BY USING

- clear, exact language
- sentences that are not wordy
- language that suits the audience

Rewrite the following directions so that they would be clear to a group of second-graders. Leave out unnecessary words and information.

     Here's how to play "Pin the Nose on the Clown." Everybody always enjoys this game. You will need a drawing of a clown face without a nose, construction paper, some pins, and a blindfold. Cut a circle from the paper for each player to make a colorful nose for the clown. You can make the nose any color you wish. Hang the clown face on a wall, blindfold the first player, and then ask the player to try to pin the nose on the clown. It's funny when someone pins the nose to the clown's ear or hair. Continue the game until everyone has had a turn. The winner is the player who comes the closest to pinning the nose where it really should be.

_____

_____

_____

_____

_____

_____

_____

Combining Sentences with Words in a Series

Good writers combine sentences to avoid repeating words.

Combine each group of sentences to make one sentence.
Write the new sentence.

1. Rey-Ling gave a party. Karen gave a party. Mitch gave a party.

   Rey-Ling, Karen, and Mitch each gave a party.

2. They met on Monday to plan the party. They met on Tuesday to plan the party.

   They met on Monday and Tuesday to plan the party.

3. They invited Tina. They invited Mark. They invited Lee.

   They invited Tina, Mark, and Lee.

4. Each guest received a paper hat. Each guest received a balloon. Each guest received a new pencil.

   Each guest received a paper hat, a balloon, a a new pencil.

5. The children played Simon Says. The children played Musical Chairs. The children played Pin the Nose on the Clown.

   The children played simon says, Musical chairs, and pin the nose on the clown.

6. Mitch taught the others a new game. Rey-Ling taught the others a new game.

   Mitch and Rey-ling each taught the others a new game.

7. Tina sang a funny song. Lee sang a funny song. Karen sang a funny song.

   Tina, Lee, and Karen each sang a funny song.

Proofreading How-to Paragraphs

Proofread the how-to paragraphs, paying special attention to punctuation marks at the end of sentences. Use Proofreading Marks to correct at least six errors.

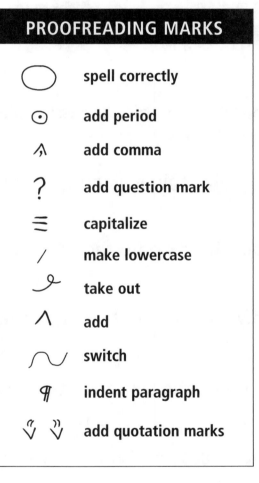

PROOFREADING MARKS	
◯	spell correctly
⊙	add period
⋀	add comma
?	add question mark
☰	capitalize
/	make lowercase
℘	take out
⋀	add
∿	switch
¶	indent paragraph
⌄ ⌄	add quotation marks

Do you enjoy collecting large or

unusually pretty leaves then you should

learn to make ink prints of leaves. Making

the prints is fun, and you'll enjoy having

pretty prints of your best leaves

The most important thing for making a leaf print is a leaf that you like.

You also need a piece of felt just a little lareger than your leaf, a smooth

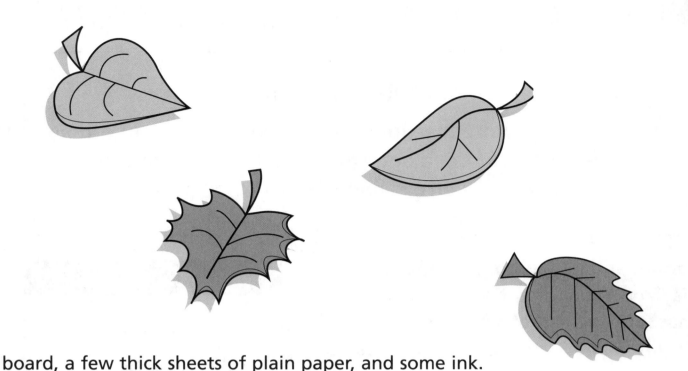

board, a few thick sheets of plain paper, and some ink.

To begin making your leaf print, place the felt on the board Carefully

pour the ink onto the felt until the hole piece is damp. With the vein-side

down, place your leaf on the felt. Cover it with a sheet of paper, and press

down on the leaf. then take away the sheet of paper, pick the leaf up, and

put it ink-side down on a clean piece of paper. Cover the leaf with another

piece of paper, and press down again When you take away the top paper

and the leaf, you'll have your own special leaf print.

Visualize Steps

Think of a sandwich you like. Visualize the ingredients and how you would make it. Then list the materials needed to make the sandwich.

_____   _____

_____   _____

_____   _____

_____   _____

_____   _____

Write a how-to paragraph for making your sandwich.

_____

_____

_____

_____

_____

_____

_____

Game Instructions

Write directions that explain to a group of second-graders how to play one of your favorite games. If you wish, use drawings as well as words to make the directions clear. Revise and proofread your work. If you want, invite a group of second-graders to play the game.

_____

_____

_____

_____

_____

_____

_____

_____

_____

Plan an Invention

With a friend or two, think of something you would like to invent. Draw a picture of your invention. Write a paragraph of instructions for using the invention.

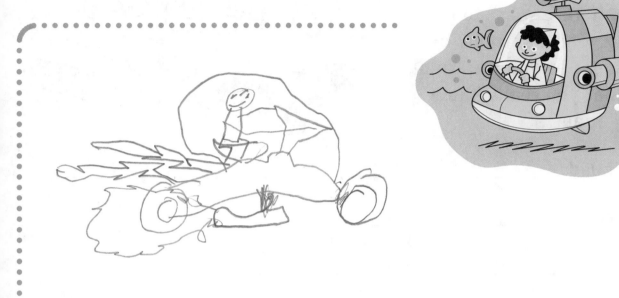

This element motercycle can control evrythind and use it to transform its self. For instne lightning can transform it into a lightning plane. And fire can turn it into a fire shotin army tank.
THE END!!!

What Do You Know How to Do?

How do you choose a topic for a how-to paragraph? Start by making a list of things you know how to do. Here is a list to get you started. Finish as many of the topic ideas as you can. Think of topics that you really know something about.

1. How to build _____

2. How to cook _____

3. How to fix _____

4. How to make _____

5. How to play _____

Show your list to a friend. Have your friend pick one topic that he or she would like to know about. Write step-by-step instructions for your friend.

_____

_____

_____

_____

_____

_____

A Practice How-to Paper

PAPIER-MÂCHÉ ZOO

Work with friends to make a papier-mâché zoo. It's easy and fun. You don't even need a lot of materials.

There are a few things you'll need to collect before you begin. They include old newspapers, a bucket, glue, water, paper cups, pipe cleaners, tempera paint, and paintbrushes.

The first step is to make the papier-mâché pulp. The pulp is soft and moist. You can shape the pulp by itself or wrap it around cups, pipe cleaners, and other objects. The objects you use depend on the shapes you want to have. When the pulp dries, it hardens. The pulp takes the shape you give it.

Tear old newspapers into small pieces. One-inch pieces work well. Put the pieces in a bucket or a pan. Now make some paste.

To make paste, mix two cups of glue with one cup of water in a cup. Stir the glue and water. Slowly, add this paste to the newspaper pieces. Be sure to add a little paste at a time. Too much paste will make the papier-mâché runny and hard to shape. Squeeze the paste and paper together until the pulp feels like soft clay.

Use reference books to find pictures of animals for your zoo. Twist pipe cleaners together to make the body for each animal.

For example, let's say you want to put a bear in your zoo. To make the bear's body, start with a straight pipe cleaner. Then bend another pipe cleaner in half. Attach it to one end of the straight pipe cleaner. Then bend another pipe cleaner in half. Attach it to the opposite end of the straight pipe cleaner. Use a fourth pipe cleaner to make the bear's head and neck. Bend the pipe cleaner in half. Twist the loose ends around one end of the straight pipe cleaner. Open the closed end of the pipe cleaner to make a head.

Press and squeeze pulp around the legs and body of the bear. Press more pulp around the neck and head. Shape small lumps of pulp to make ears, a nose, and a tail for the bear. Add pulp until the bear is the size you want. Then leave the bear in an open place for two or more days to dry.

When the bear is dry, paint the bear. Use paint to add eyes and a nose. You can glue decorations onto your bear, too.

Together, you and your friends can make a large zoo. You might even want to use papier-mâché pulp to make homes for your animals. Find a large cardboard box. Use pulp to make caves, swimming pools, and other animal homes inside the box. Paint the homes and let them dry. Finally, add your animals and give your zoo a name.

Respond to the Practice Paper

Write your answers to the following questions or directions.

1. What does this how-to paper teach you to do?

   _____

   _____

2. What materials do you need to do this project?

   _____

   _____

3. After you have collected your materials, what is the first thing you should do?

   _____

   _____

4. Why can't the pulp be runny?

   _____

   _____

5. Write a paragraph to describe a papier-mâché animal you would like to make. On a separate piece of paper, draw a picture to go with your paragraph.

   _____

   _____

   _____

Analyze the Practice Paper

Read "Papier-Mâché Zoo" again. As you read, think about why the writer wrote this paper. Was the writer able to do what he or she planned to do? Write your answers to the following questions.

1. What makes this model an example of a how-to paper?

   _____

   _____

2. What is the first thing the writer tells you to do before you begin to make a papier-mâché zoo?

   _____

   _____

3. Why do you think the writer lists the materials you need for this project?

   _____

   _____

4. Why does the writer use sequence words, such as *first*, *now*, and *then*?

   _____

   _____

5. Read the sixth paragraph again. On a separate piece of paper, draw a picture of the bear's pipe-cleaner body. Do you think the writer did a good job describing the steps?

   _____

   _____

   _____

Writing Assignment

Think about something you want to tell others how to do. Use this writing plan to help you write a first draft on the next page.

Tell what you are explaining to someone.

▼

List the materials someone will need to do this project.

▼

Write the steps someone should follow in order. Number the steps.

▼

Write some sequence words you can use in your paper.

First Draft

TIPS FOR WRITING A HOW-TO PAPER:

- Choose a single topic or project.
- Focus on a plan.
  1. Think of all of the materials someone will need.
  2. Think of all of the steps someone must follow.

- Use sequence words in your directions. A thesaurus will help you find words you need.

Use your writing plan as a guide as you write your first draft of a how-to paper. Include a catchy title.

_____

_____

_____

_____

_____

_____

_____

_____

_____

(Continue on your own paper.)

Revise the Draft

Use the chart below to help you revise your draft. Check YES or NO to answer each question in the chart. If you answer NO, make notes to remind yourself how you can revise, or change, your writing to improve it.

Question	YES ✔	NO ✔	If the answer is NO, what will you do to improve your writing?
Does your paper explain how to do something specific?			
Do you use the first paragraph to introduce the project?			
Do you describe all of the steps someone needs to follow?			
Do you write the steps in the order they should happen?			
Is each step written clearly so that it is easy to follow?			
Do you use sequence words to help make the directions easy to follow?			
Have you corrected mistakes in spelling, grammar, and punctuation?			

Use the notes in your chart and your writing plan to revise your draft.

Writing Report Card

Read your revised draft again or ask someone else to read it. Have the person who reads your paper complete the following Report Card. Revise your paper until you have no less than a Very Good Score for each item.

Title of paper: _____

Purpose of paper: ___*This paper is a how-to paper.*_____

Person who scores the paper: _____

Score	Writing Goals
	Does the paper explain how to do something specific?
	Does the first paragraph explain what the paper will be about?
	Are the steps in order?
	Are there sequence words that make the directions easy to follow?
	Are there enough details for the reader to follow each step?
	Are the story's grammar, spelling, and punctuation correct?

☺ Excellent Score   ☆ Very Good Score   + Good Score
✔ Acceptable Score   − Needs Improvement

UNIT 3: Fable

HOW MUCH DO YOU KNOW?

Read the fable. Then answer the questions.

Dove was in her bedroom dressing for Wren's party. How proud she was of her snowy white dress! It had to be the most beautiful dress at the party. Dove turned around and around, admiring her reflection in the mirror. "How lovely I look!" she cried. Then her wing bumped a bottle of ink that was sitting on the desk. The bottle turned over. Splash! The front of Dove's dress was covered with an inky black stain.

MORAL:
Be proud of yourself, but do not be more proud than you should be.

1.   What is the setting of the fable?

_____

2.   What lesson does the fable teach?

_____

_____

3.   What else might Dove say at the beginning of the story?
      Circle your answer.

        a. "I hope someone at the party will dance with me."

        b. "I know I'll be the most beautiful bird at the party."

        c. "I don't care what I wear to this party."

        d. "I hope this blue dress will fit me."

Analyzing a Fable

> **A FABLE**
> - teaches a lesson
> - has characters, a setting, and a plot
> - ends with a moral

Read the fable. Then answer the questions.

Deep in the outback of Australia lived Emu and Bowerbird. Emu was sad. He could run as swiftly as the wind on his long legs, but try as he might, he could not fly. Bowerbird, too, felt sad. He could soar high and far with his strong wings, but he could not run at all.

"How lucky you are," sighed Emu, "to fly like that!"

Bowerbird was surprised. "You are the lucky one, for see how you run!"

The two birds thought and thought, and at last they agreed upon a fine plan. "I'll teach you," they both said, "and you teach me!"

That is what they did. After many lessons and much practice, Emu became the only bird in his family who could fly. Bowerbird discovered that running was not so difficult after all.

MORAL:

With a little help from a friend, you can do anything.

1. What is the setting of the fable? _____

2. Who are the characters? _____

3. What problem do the characters have? _____

_____

4. How do they solve the problem? _____

_____

5. What lesson does the fable teach? _____

_____

6. What do you think would be a good title for the fable?

_____

Evaluating Ideas to Support a Conclusion

> **TO WRITE A FABLE, GOOD WRITERS**
> - choose a conclusion
> - evaluate possible events and ideas
> - select the facts that best support the conclusion

A. Underline the idea that best supports the conclusion. On the lines write another statement that would help a reader draw that conclusion.

Conclusion: Mrs. Mason will receive the letter today.

1.   (a)   It was almost time for lunch to be served.
       (b)   Mrs. Mason's mailbox is near her steps.
       (c)   Mrs. Mason watched eagerly up the street, looking for the mail carrier.

2. _____

   _____

B. Imagine that you are going to write a paragraph based on the conclusion given below. Write *yes* beside each statement you will use to support the conclusion. Write *no* beside each statement that does not support the conclusion.

Conclusion: Yoshiko will take good care of her new puppy.

3. _____ Dogs needs lots of room to run and play.
4. _____ Yoshiko is a very dependable person.
5. _____ A puppy is a lot of trouble.
6. _____ Yoshiko bought a book about pet care.
7. _____ Yoshiko has never had a dog before.
8. _____ Yoshiko takes good care of her other pets.
9. _____ She understands that puppies need love and attention.

Storytelling: Dialogue and Characters

> **GOOD WRITERS CREATE INTERESTING CHARACTERS THROUGH**
> - dialogue, or conversation
> - vivid details

A. Read the paragraph. Then answer the questions.

Libby sat down beside the new girl in her class and smiled. "Hi, I'm Libby," she said. "Want to play with me at recess?"

1. What does the paragraph reveal about the kind of person Libby is?

_____

2. What details about her actions does the writer use to reveal her character?

_____

3. How does the dialogue reveal her character?

_____

_____

B. Use the information below to continue the story about Libby. Add details and dialogue to show what the characters are like.

The new girl's name is Allison. She thinks no one will want to play with her because she has to stay in her wheelchair all the time. Libby is sure Allison will have many friends. She suggests that they play catch with the big blue ball.

_____

_____

_____

Avoiding Wordy Language

> Good writers say what they mean
> in as few words as possible.

Rewrite the story. Take out the underlined words or replace them with fewer words that mean the same thing.

    Dove was <u>putting on her clothes and getting ready</u> for Wren's party. How <u>puffed up and proud</u> she was of her snowy white dress! It might possibly be the most beautiful outfit of all <u>the group that had been invited to the party</u>. Dove turned around and around. She admired the <u>reflection of herself in the mirror</u>. "How lovely I look!" she cried. <u>Just about that time</u>, her wing bumped a bottle of ink that was sitting on the desk. The <u>little bottle of ink</u> turned over. Splash! Down the front of <u>the white dress that Dove was wearing</u> went an inky black stain.

MORAL:

Be proud of yourself, but <u>be careful not to be</u> more proud than you should be.

_____

_____

_____

_____

_____

_____

Proofreading a Fable

Proofread the beginning of the fable, paying special attention to quotation marks and commas in dialogue. Use the Proofreading Marks to correct at least seven errors.

PROOFREADING MARKS	
◯	spell correctly
⊙	add period
⋏	add comma
?	add question mark
≡	capitalize
/	make lowercase
৶	take out
∧	add
∿	switch
¶	indent paragraph
⌄ ⌄	add quotation marks

Baby Chick peered through the tall grass at the edge of the pond. His freinds Little Duck and Little Swan splashed happily in the water.

Come on in, Baby Chick!" called Little Duck.

"Yes, added Little Swan. The water's nice and warm today."

Little Duck quacked "Watch me do a trick!" Then he put his head under the water and turned a somersault

Baby Chick sighed. "I wish I could do that" he answered. "Swimming looks like such fun. Look at my feet, though. Yours are webbed, but mine just have little chicken toes

"Don't worry," laughed Little Swan. "I'm sure you can learn to swim anyway. Look at this!" He proudly traced a figure ate in the water.

Read a Fable

Read several fables in library books. Choose a favorite fable. Write a paragraph that tells the setting, characters, and plot of the fable. Then write the moral.

_____

_____

_____

_____

_____

_____

_____

_____

MORAL:

_____

_____

_____

Write a Story Ending

Reread the story of Dove. With a friend, write a story ending that tells what Dove did about the stain on her dress. Revise your work. Use dialogue and vivid details.

Dove was in her bedroom dressing for Wren's party. How proud she was of her snowy white dress! It had to be the most beautiful dress at the party. Dove turned around and around, admiring her reflection in the mirror. "How lovely I look!" she cried. Then her wing bumped a bottle of ink that was sitting on the desk. The bottle turned over. Splash! The front of Dove's dress was covered with an inky black stain.

Write a Fable

Fables usually have animal characters. The animals are often enemies or unlikely companions. Read the pairs of characters in the chart. Add some characters of your own.

With a friend, choose a pair of characters from the chart. Together, write a fable about the characters. Be sure that it ends with a moral.

NATURAL ENEMIES	OPPOSITES
cat and bird wolf and chicken	elephant (big) and ant (small) parrot (brightly colored) and dove (gray)

_____

_____

_____

_____

_____

_____

_____

_____

_____

_____

_____

_____

A Practice Fable

THE ANTS AND THE DOVE

A Fable by Aesop

Ant looked at the seed that lay at her feet. On a spring day, that seed would be easy to carry home. But on a day like today, she might as well try to push a mountain. "My, it's hot," Ant complained softly. "My feet are killing me."

"I agree," said Ant Two. "Sun has been up all morning. Doesn't he have anything better to do? Shine, shine, shine. Goodness, I've had quite enough."

"That's Sun for you. That's his only job. He shines while we work," said Ant.

"Hmmph," said Ant Two. "Even in winter, he shines as though he has nothing better to do. It's not fair, I say. He should have to drag seeds across this dusty meadow at the end of summer."

Ant chuckled. "I'd like to see that," she said. "Imagine that big ball of gas rolling seeds across this field." She got ready to start work again. "Well, we can't stand here all day. It's not getting any cooler, you know. Let's go, shall we?"

"Oh, please, not yet," cried Ant Two. "I can't go on without a drink of water. My antennae tell me there is a river nearby."

Ant dropped her seed again. She waved her antennae. "You're right. I smell it, too. It's coming from that direction," she said as she pointed to a family of trees. "Let's both go."

Ant and Ant Two stepped over and under blades of dry grass. They waved their antennae, searching for signs of hungry lizards. But nothing moved, not even the wind.

The trees stood along the river's bank. They looked like guards outside a castle. The trees threw their shadows across the river, shading it from Sun. Ant and Ant Two stopped to stare. "It's beautiful, isn't it, Ant?"

"Oh, yes. But be careful. Walk softly. The soil is dry. It may spill if you walk heavily."

Ant's warning came too late. Ant Two tumbled down the bank. She plopped into the water and was carried away. "Ant!" she cried behind her. "Help me, please! I can't swim!"

Ant stood on the bank watching her friend float away. "This is terrible," she thought. "What can I do?" She moved quickly along the bank, looking for a twig or vine she could use to rescue her friend.

Downstream, Dove slept quietly at the top of a dusty oak tree. She opened one eye when she heard something slapping the water. The noise traveled with the river. Soon, Dove could see an ant trying to swim. Dove cut a leaf from the tree and let it fall. It landed just as Ant Two floated by. Ant Two jumped aboard, gasping for air. She looked up to see Dove. Dove nodded and closed her eyes.

Ant pulled the leaf and Ant Two from the water. They rested on the bank while Ant Two told her story. Ant Two added lots of details to her story, so Ant listened for a long time. Ant Two was still talking when Ant warned her to be quiet. Ant smelled a human.

The human carried a net. Ant and Ant Two looked at each other. They wiggled their antennae. They smelled danger.

Ant and Ant Two followed the human. He stopped beneath the oak tree where Dove slept quietly. She had not heard the human. Ant and Ant Two looked at each other. They knew what they had to do.

As the human began to throw his net, Ant and Ant Two stung his legs. The human jumped and began scratching fiercely. The noise woke Dove. She glanced to the ground where Ant and Ant Two stood waving. Dove nodded thankfully, opened her wings, and flew away.

Respond to the Practice Paper

Write your answers to the following questions or directions.

1. A fable is a story that teaches a lesson. What is the lesson of this story?

   _____

   _____

2. The animals in fables often act like humans. Name one way the animals in this story act like humans.

   _____

   _____

3. How would you describe the setting for this story?

   _____

   _____

4. Write a paragraph to summarize this story. Use these questions to help you write your summary:
   - What are the main ideas in the story?
   - How does the story end?
   - What lesson does this story teach?

   _____

   _____

   _____

   _____

   _____

   _____

   _____

Analyze the Practice Paper

Read the fable "The Ants and the Dove" again. As you read, think about how the writer wrote the story. Answer the following questions or directions.

1. What does the writer do to make this story fun to read?

    _____

    _____

    _____

2. How does the writer make the characters seem human?

    _____

    _____

    _____

3. Name two problems the writer uses to make the story exciting.

    _____

    _____

    _____

4. How does the writer solve these problems?

    _____

    _____

    _____

5. Why is dialogue, or conversation, important to this story?

    _____

    _____

    _____

Writing Assignment

Sometimes stories help us learn about ourselves. They help us think about what we can be or do. Think about writing a fable. What lesson would you like to teach? What animals will you use as characters in your story? It might help you to think about the traits we sometimes give to animals. For example, some people say dogs are faithful or cats are curious. Use this writing plan to help you write a first draft on the next page.

What is the lesson of the fable?

▼

Who are the animal characters?

▼

What problem will the characters have?

▼

How will the characters solve their problem? List what will happen in the story.

First Draft

TIPS FOR WRITING A FABLE:

- Think about the lesson you want your fable to teach.
- Give your animal characters human traits.
- Think about where the story will happen.
- Give your characters a problem.
- Write what happens to the characters in order from beginning to end.

Use your writing plan as a guide as you write your first draft of a fable. Include a catchy title.

_____

_____

_____

_____

_____

_____

_____

(Continue on your own paper.)

Revise the Draft

Use the chart below to help you revise your draft. Check YES or NO to answer each question in the chart. If you answer NO, make notes to remind yourself how you can revise, or change, your writing to improve it.

Question	YES ✔	NO ✔	If the answer is NO, what will you do to improve your writing?
Does your fable teach a lesson?			
Do your animal characters have human traits?			
Does your fable have a strong beginning?			
Do your characters have a problem?			
Do you describe events in the order they happen?			
Do the characters solve their problem?			
Do you include important details that help the reader imagine the characters and their problem?			
Have you corrected mistakes in spelling, grammar, and punctuation?			

Use the notes in your chart and your writing plan to revise your draft.

Writing Report Card

Read your revised draft again or ask someone else to read it. Have the person who reads your paper complete the following Report Card. Revise your paper until you have no less than a Very Good Score for each item.

Title of paper: _____

Purpose of paper: _*This paper is a fable.*_____

Person who scores the paper: _____

Score	Writing Goals
	Does this story teach a lesson?
	Do the animal characters in this story have human traits?
	Do the characters have a problem they must solve?
	Are events in the story described in the order they happen?
	Are there enough details to describe each event?
	Are there a variety of sentences that make the story interesting?
	Are the story's grammar, spelling, and punctuation correct?

☺ Excellent Score　　☆ Very Good Score　　+ Good Score
✔ Acceptable Score　　− Needs Improvement

UNIT 4: Comparative Writing

HOW MUCH DO YOU KNOW?

Write the number of each sentence below in the correct column to show whether it belongs in a paragraph of comparison or a paragraph of contrast.

1. The Amazon River is the longest in South America, while the Missouri River is the longest in North America.

2. Instead of traveling across plains, the Amazon travels through a rain forest.

3. Both the Amazon and the Missouri give travelers dramatic views of nature.

4. Unlike the Missouri, which flows to a river, the Amazon flows to an ocean.

5. Ships travel on both the Amazon and the Missouri Rivers.

Paragraph of Comparison   **Paragraph of Contrast**

_____   _____

_____   _____

_____   _____

_____   _____

_____   _____

Answer the questions.

6. In the sentences above, which signal word calls attention to details that are alike?

_____

7. Which signal words call attention to details that are different?

_____

Analyzing Paragraphs of Comparison and Contrast

A paragraph of comparison tells how two people,
two places, or two things are like each other.

A paragraph of contrast tells how two subjects
are different from each other.

A. Write the number of each sentence below in the correct column to
show whether it belongs in a paragraph of comparison or a paragraph
of contrast.

1. Guatemala and Costa Rica are both Central American nations.

2. Like Guatemala, Costa Rica grows coffee, bananas, and grains.

3. Costa Rica's money is called a colón, but Guatemala's is the quetzal.

4. Unlike Costa Rica, Guatemala has many people who speak Indian
   languages.

5. The countries have the same national language, Spanish.

6. Instead of bordering Mexico, Costa Rica borders Panama and Nicaragua.

Paragraph of Comparison   **Paragraph of Contrast**

_____   _____

_____   _____

_____   _____

_____   _____

_____   _____

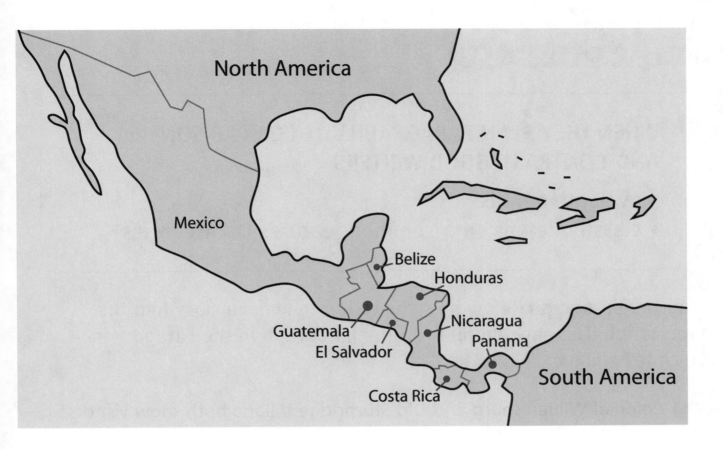

North America

Mexico

Belize

Honduras

Guatemala

Nicaragua

El Salvador

Panama

Costa Rica

South America

B. Answer the questions.

7. In the sentences at left, which signal words call attention to details that are alike?

_____

8. Which signal words call attention to details that are different?

_____

Evaluating to Compare and Contrast

WHEN THEY PLAN PARAGRAPHS OF COMPARISON AND CONTRAST, GOOD WRITERS

- evaluate details
- classify details with common features in categories

Read the paragraph. Show how the writer may have classified the information. List each detail from the paragraph in the category in which it belongs.

Colonial Williamsburg and Old Sturbridge Village both show visitors what life was like in the past. Colonial Williamsburg demonstrates life in the 1700s, and Old Sturbridge Village is a re-creation of a New England village of about 1830. Both have many shops and other buildings that are open to

COLONIAL WILLIAMSBURG	BOTH PLACES	OLD STURBRIDGE VILLAGE

tourists. Since Williamsburg was an important city in the colony of Virginia, the restored buildings there include the Capitol, the Governor's Palace, and several elegant houses. On the other hand, Old Sturbridge Village gives visitors a taste of life in the country. It includes a farm, a sawmill, and a mill for grinding grain. Popular attractions in both Old Sturbridge Village and Colonial Williamsburg are the demonstrations of crafts that were necessary to life in those times.

Using Formal and Informal Language

Good writers use formal language to give information.

Rewrite each sentence, replacing informal language with formal language.

1. The Hermitage is a great big house.

   _____

2. Andrew Jackson hung out there for 26 years.

   _____

3. Jackson's wife gave the okay for the site for the house.

   _____

4. Jackson hadn't been elected president yet when he built the house in 1819.

   _____

5. The view from the house is pretty nice.

   _____

6. You can see swell green hills from up there.

   _____

7. A big fire just about ruined the house in 1834.

   _____

8. Jackson didn't waste any time rebuilding it.

   _____

9. He gave lots of parties and invited a bunch of people.

   _____

Adding Describing Words to Sentences

> Good writers choose the right describing words to create clear, strong pictures.

Replace each word in parentheses ( ) with a vivid and exact describing word. Use words from the box.

lovely	frantic	peaceful	colorful	glistening
ear-splitting	towering	bustling	gentle	
silent	fabulous	precious	longed-for	

1. The valley was a _____ place.
   (quiet)

2. Nestled in the _____ Rockies, it was blanketed with
   (high)

   _____ snow much of the year.
   (shiny)

3. In the summer, green grass and _____ flowers covered
   (pretty)

   the hillsides.

4. Deer grazed there as _____ breezes whispered.
   (slow)

5. Then one day, _____ gold was discovered in the
   (valuable)

   _____ valley.
   (nice)

6. Thousands of people rushed to find _____ riches.
   (great)

7. Suddenly, Caribou turned into a _____ city.
   (busy)

8. The valley was filled with the _____ noise of
   (loud)

   _____ miners searching for gold.
   (eager)

9. Before long, all the _____ gold was gone.
   (wanted)

10. Now Caribou is _____ again, only a ghost town.
    (quiet)

Proofreading Paragraphs of Comparison and Contrast

> **PROOFREADING HINT**
>
> To be a good proofreader, look for one type of error at a time. For example, proofread once for capitalization errors, once for punctuation errors, and once for spelling errors.

Proofread the paragraphs of comparison and contrast, paying special attention to capital letters in the names of places. Use the Proofreading Marks to correct at least seven errors.

PROOFREADING MARKS	
⬭	spell correctly
⊙	add period
⋏	add comma
?	add question mark
☰	capitalize
/	make lowercase
℘	take out
∧	add
∿	switch
¶	indent paragraph
⌄ ⌄	add quotation marks

Texas and New mexico are

neighboring states, and in many weighs

they are alike. Of course, they share a

common border. Both states have large

areas of land that are dry and flat, and

both states have mountains. New Mexico's

capital, santa fe, is not the state's largest city, and Austin, the capital of

Texas, is much smaller than Houston, dallas, or San Antonio.

Although new Mexico and Texas have much in common, they are different in many ways. Some American Indians live in texas, but they make up a much larger portion of the population of New Mexico. The land is also different. Unlike Texas, New mexico has areas of true desert. Also, the rocky Mountains slice through central New Mexico, giving the State large areas of green forests. The mountains of texas, in the area called Big Bend, are much drier and are not forested.

Make a Chart of Comparison and Contrast

Think about your town and a neighboring town. Fill in the chart showing how your town and the neighboring town are alike and how they are different. Then, write a paragraph comparing and contrasting the two places.

HOW THE TOWNS ARE ALIKE	HOW THE TOWNS ARE DIFFERENT

Write from a Set of Topic Ideas

Read the list of paired topic ideas. The two animals or objects in each pair are alike—but not completely. How are they similar? How are they different? Choose one pair and write a paragraph of comparison and contrast.

helicopter, jet   frog, toad   cello, violin

horse, donkey   bicycle, motorcycle   butterfly, moth

A helicopter and a jet are similar but not the same. A jet is propeled by a jet enghin. And a helecopter is propeled by a moterto. But relise on its roter blades. to stay in the air. Both are air craft, but the jet goes much faster!

Compare and Contrast People

To help find people to compare and contrast, complete the pairs of phrases below. Write the opposite of the underlined word to finish the second phrase in each pair. Then, write a pair of your own. Select one of the pairs. With a friend, write a paragraph to compare and contrast the people.

my <u>aunt</u> and my _____

a popular <u>actor</u> and a popular _____

a <u>sleepy</u> friend and a _____ friend

_____

_____

_____

_____

_____

_____

A Practice Compare-and-Contrast Paper

ALLIGATORS AND CROCODILES

Do you watch adventure movies? You probably know the kind I mean. Somewhere in the world, science experiments go bad. Meat-eating dinosaurs chase humans across the screen. Giant gorillas step on cars and buildings. The animals aren't real, of course, but it's easy to forget that. The fierce-looking animals and the noise keep you waiting to see who will leave the scene alive. For two exciting hours, you forget that you are watching a movie.

Some of the big stars of action movies are life-size reptiles. Alligators and crocodiles are two examples. To some people, they seem like the same animal. It's easy to understand why. In one quick glance, people see long bodies, tough skin, and sharp teeth. But there's more to these reptiles than you might think.

Let's take a closer look at both of these animals. We'll begin with the American Alligator.

When it is grown, the American Alligator is blackish in color. It has a wide, flat snout. When its mouth is closed, the upper jaw hides the teeth in the lower jaw. Teeth in the upper jaw remain visible. Full grown, alligators can be more than 15 feet long and weigh about 500 pounds. When they walk slowly, alligators drag their tails. If they're in a hurry, they can "high walk." That means they walk on their toes. The hind feet and tail leave the ground. This lets alligators run up to 30 miles per hour. They live in and near freshwater lakes, rivers, and swamps. Sometimes, they live in water that's a little saltier than most freshwater.

Now let's look at the American Crocodile. As an adult, it is olive-brown. It has a long, narrow snout. When its mouth is closed, teeth in both jaws remain visible. The fourth tooth on the lower jaw sticks out. American Crocodiles are some of the world's largest crocodiles. Some can grow more than 15 feet long and weigh as much as 450 pounds. They live in freshwater and where saltwater and freshwater meet.

We've talked about how these reptiles look and where they live. Now let's talk about what they eat and where they lay their eggs.

Alligators eat different kinds of foods, including fish, frogs, turtles, snakes, water birds, deer, and other alligators. First, they drown their prey. Then, they use their teeth, slap the prey against the water, or drag the prey around to break it into bite-sized pieces.

Crocodiles eat fish but may also eat any animal that comes too close. They usually drown the prey first and then swallow it whole.

When it's time to mate, the female alligator builds a nest. She uses plants to build mounds that rise out of the water. These mounds are the nests. Each mound can hold about 30 eggs. The eggs hatch in about two months. But baby alligators stay near their mothers a lot longer. Some stay near their mothers for more than two years.

Female crocodiles build nests, too, but not mounds. They dig holes in sand or mud. Then they lay between 30 and 60 eggs. The eggs take about three months to hatch. Baby crocodiles move away from their mothers a few days after birth.

Why do people who make movies use alligators and crocodiles as their models? Maybe it's because these reptiles are large and powerful. Or maybe it's because they have lots of teeth and unusual behaviors. Whatever the reason, alligators and crocodiles are big movie stars.

Respond to the Practice Paper

Which two your answers to the following questions or directions.

1. Which two animals does this paper compare and contrast?

   _____

   _____

2. Summarize the paper by making a chart. Use the chart below to list ways alligators and crocodiles are alike and different.

A COMPARE-AND-CONTRAST CHART FOR ALLIGATORS AND CROCODILES

How Alligators and Crocodiles Are Alike	How Alligators and Crocodiles Are Different

Analyze the Practice Paper

Read "Alligators and Crocodiles" again. As you read, think about how the writer organized information in this paper. Write your answers to the following questions.

1. Most of the time, a writer tells what a paper will be about in the first paragraph. Why do you think this writer begins this paper by talking about action movies?

   _____

   _____

2. How did the writer let you know that this paper was going to be about real alligators and crocodiles?

   _____

   _____

3. First, the writer describes the way alligators and crocodiles look. How does the writer let you know that the main idea is about to change?

   _____

   _____

4. In the fourth paragraph, the writer describes alligators. In the fifth paragraph, the writer describes crocodiles. What does the writer describe in the seventh and eighth paragraphs? Why do you think the writer organized the paper this way?

   _____

   _____

5. Why do you think the writer talks about movies again in the last paragraph?

   _____

   _____

Writing Assignment

When writers compare and contrast two or more things, their main ideas are the important ways that the things are alike and different. Then writers use details to support each main idea. Think about two animals you would like to compare and contrast. Think about writing a paper about them. Use this writing plan to help you write a first draft on page 86.

Choose two animals you want to compare and contrast. Call them Animal A and Animal B.

A = _____   B = _____

Use reference materials such as the encyclopedia to learn more about the animals you chose. Learn about how they look, where they live, and what they eat.

The main ideas are written outside each set of circles below. For each main idea, list what is true only about Animal A in the A circle. List what is true only about Animal B in the B circle. List what is true about both animals where the two circles overlap.

MAIN IDEA:
How they look

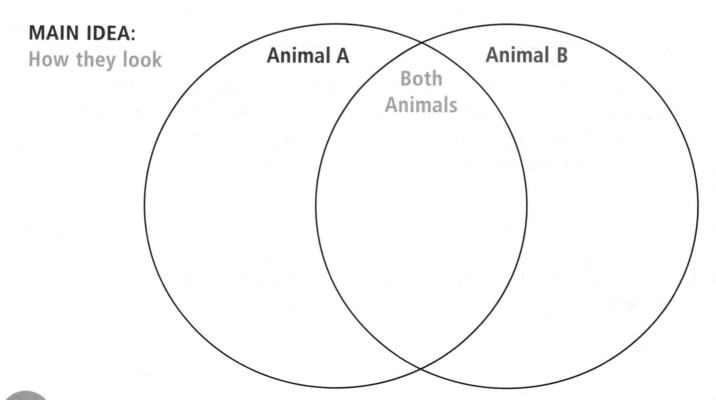

Animal A   Both Animals   Animal B

MAIN IDEA:
Where they live

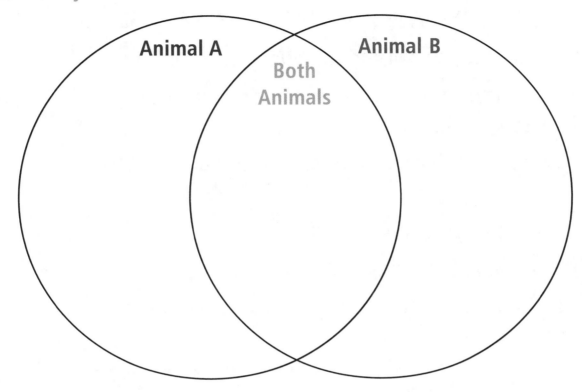

MAIN IDEA:
What they eat

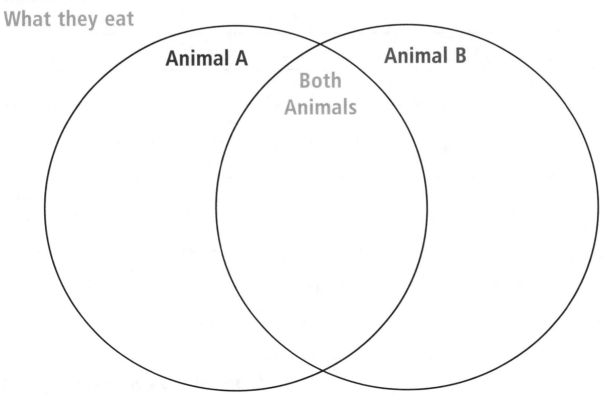

First Draft

TIPS FOR WRITING A PAPER THAT COMPARES AND CONTRASTS:

- Use reference materials to collect information.
- Use the information you collect to choose the most important main ideas.
- Write an introduction that tells the reader what your paper is about.
- Explain how the animals are alike.
- Explain how the animals are different.
- Write sentences that help your reader move from one main idea to another.

Use your writing plan as a guide as you write your first draft of a compare-and-contrast paper. Include a catchy title.

_____

_____

_____

_____

_____

_____

_____

_____

_____

(Continue on your own paper.)

Revise the Draft

Use the chart below to help you revise your draft. Check YES or NO to answer each question in the chart. If you answer NO, make notes to remind yourself how you can revise, or change, your writing to improve it.

Question	YES ✔	NO ✔	If the answer is NO, what will you do to improve your writing?
Do you introduce the animals you will write about in the first paragraph?			
Do you tell how two animals are alike?			
Do you tell how two animals are different?			
Do you have more than one main idea?			
Do you organize the main ideas into paragraphs?			
Do you use details to support each main idea?			
Do you summarize the main ideas of your paper in your conclusion?			
Have you corrected mistakes in spelling, grammar, and punctuation?			

Use the notes in your chart and your writing plan to revise your draft.

Writing Report Card

Read your revised draft again or ask someone else to read it. Have the person who reads your paper complete the following Report Card. Revise your paper until you have no less than a Very Good Score for each item.

Title of paper: _____

Purpose of paper: _This paper tells how two animals are alike and different._

Person who scores the paper: _____

Score	Writing Goals
	Does the first paragraph tell what the paper is about?
	Does the paper tell how two animals are alike?
	Does the paper tell how two animals are different?
	Is there more than one main idea?
	Are the main ideas organized into paragraphs?
	Are there enough details to support each main idea?
	Are the paragraphs in an order that makes sense?
	Does the last paragraph summarize what the paper is about?
	Are the paper's grammar, spelling, and punctuation correct?

☺ Excellent Score ☆ Very Good Score + Good Score
✔ Acceptable Score − Needs Improvement

UNIT 5: Descriptive Writing

HOW MUCH DO YOU KNOW?

Yellowstone National Park has some of the strangest scenery. Great Fountain Geyser sometimes shoots water higher than a twenty-story building. Yellowstone Lake is our country's largest high-altitude lake. Its sparkling water seems shinier than a mirror. The smell of pine trees fills the air. Yellowstone has a deep canyon, but the Grand Canyon in Arizona is deeper. In addition, the park has about 10,000 hot springs with steam rising up to the sky.

1. What is the topic sentence of the paragraph?

   _____

   _____

2. Which detail appeals to the sense of smell?

   _____

   _____

3. Which details could be used to describe the geyser? (Circle all that apply.)

   a. spray of warm water on your face

   b. shoots water as high as the treetops

   c. smell of chocolate syrup

   d. with a hissing sound the water sprays into the air

   e. bright red and purple

Analyzing a Descriptive Paragraph

> **A DESCRIPTIVE PARAGRAPH**
> - has a topic sentence that tells what will be described
> - gives details that appeal to the reader's senses
> - groups details that belong together
> - paints a vivid word picture

Read the descriptive paragraph below. Then answer the questions.

The wintry scene looked like an artist's dream. Horses clip-clopped along on the hard-packed road. Their harness bells jingled. Passengers in their carriages breathed the icy air and snuggled deeper into bright red and purple blankets. The road sloped upward between rows of towering pines. Their branches drooped with snow. Crowning the top of the hill, the castle poked its cold stone towers into the gray sky.

1. Draw a line under the topic sentence of the paragraph.

2. What is the purpose of the topic sentence?

_____

3. Which details appeal to the sense of hearing?

_____

4. Which details appeal to the sense of touch?

_____

5. Which details appeal to the sense of sight?

_____

6. In what way does the writer group the details?

_____

Observing Details

IN A DESCRIPTIVE PARAGRAPH, GOOD WRITERS
- group details in a way that makes sense, such as front to back or top to bottom
- organize groups of details in a way that makes sense

Study the groups of details in the chart below. Then use the details to finish writing the paragraph.

OUTSIDE THE HOUSE	ABOVE THE HOUSE	INSIDE THE HOUSE
shadows	crows circling	cold, damp air
broken windows	drooping branches	old, musty smell
overgrown with weeds	dark cloud	cobwebs
		creaking door

Scott approached the old house cautiously. It was half hidden by

_____. The _____ on each side of the

front door told him that no one had lived here in a long time. The flowerbeds were _____ , giving the house a sad and

neglected look. Glancing up, Scott saw _____ around

the crooked chimney. _____ from huge trees brushed the

roof. In the sky, a _____ slipped by. Timidly, Scott pushed

open the door. His face felt the _____ _____ , and his

nose quivered at the _____ . Thick _____ covered

the old furniture. From somewhere overhead, Scott heard a

_____ .

Using Metaphors and Similes

Good writers create vivid word pictures by comparing two things that are not usually thought of as being alike.

Similes use the word *like* or *as* in the comparison. Metaphors do not.

A. Read the paragraph. Then complete the sentences.

The deep lake was a golden mirror reflecting the setting sun. Like a large ball of orange wax slowly melting, the sun slipped below the treetops. Across the water, a row of mountain peaks raised jagged teeth to the sky. Beyond the mountains, the sunset blazed like a pink and orange flame.

1. One metaphor compares _____ to _____.

2. Another metaphor compares _____ to _____.

3. One simile compares _____ to _____.

4. Another simile compares _____ to _____.

B. Complete each metaphor or simile.

5. (metaphor) The white clouds were _____.

6. (simile) The warm breeze was like _____.

7. (metaphor) The rows of corn were _____.

8. (simile) The falling autumn leaves were like_____.

Avoiding Run-on Sentences

> Good writers avoid run-on sentences.

Correct each run-on sentence.

1. Our boat chugged into the bay we saw that the opposite shore was covered by solid ice.

   _____

   _____

2. The mountain of ice was a glacier it rose straight up out of the water.

   _____

   _____

3. I moved out onto the deck an icy wind blistered my face.

   _____

4. Our boat chugged nearer to the wall of ice the wind grew even colder.

   _____

   _____

5. Now I could see jagged pieces of ice floating in the water some had furry passengers.

   _____

   _____

6. The passengers were soft-eyed seals they stared at me without fear.

   _____

7. We drew close to the glacier then we heard a loud rumbling.

   _____

8. A chunk of ice fell from the glacier it dropped into the water.

   _____

Proofreading a Descriptive Paragraph

Proofread the descriptive paragraph, paying special attention to the agreement of subjects and verbs. Use the Proofreading Marks to correct at least seven errors.

PROOFREADING MARKS	
◯	spell correctly
⊙	add period
⋀	add comma
?	add question mark
≡	capitalize
/	make lowercase
℘	take out
∧	add
∿	switch
¶	indent paragraph
⌄ ⌄	add quotation marks

On this sunny day, the crowded beach is as busy as a school playground during recess. Far from the waves, families spreads blankets on the sand and share picnic lunches. A child dig in the sand while his older brother and sister toss a beach ball back and forth. A little nearer the water, huge umbrellas sprout like brightly-colored mushrooms. Men and women stretches out in the shade to read or nap. At the edge of the ocean, a small girl build a sand castle. Her brother look for pretty shells and helps her decorate the castle walls The soft sand and shallow water attract children of all ages. They runs and splash where the water laps the beech. Farther from shore strong swimmers rides the waves. Floating on there backs, they look like playful dolphins. Out where the waves spray white foam, a few surfboards skim across the water. The boards rises and plunge on the waves like crazy elevators.

Writing Metaphors and Similes

Find a picture of a pretty scene in an old magazine. Cut out the picture and paste it in the space below. Under the picture, write some metaphors and similes that describe the picture.

_____

_____

_____

_____

_____

_____

Observe Details

Observe details about your school. Complete the chart by grouping the details according to where they are located.

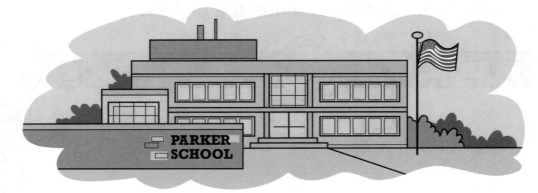

OUTSIDE THE SCHOOL	ABOVE THE SCHOOL	INSIDE THE SCHOOL

Use the details in the chart to write a descriptive paragraph about your school.

_____

_____

_____

_____

_____

_____

A Practice Descriptive Story

FIRST DAY AT THE BEACH

Miss and Match were puppies. They watched as we put their blue water jug, bowls, food, and towels in the car. Miss and Match knew they were going somewhere special.

We parked in a small lot by the dock. Miss and Match leaped from the back seat. So far, they didn't notice anything unusual. But as soon as their paws touched the sand, the dogs froze. They knew. They had never been here before.

The sand was almost white. The water's color changed all the time. Sometimes it looked blue. Sometimes it looked gray. The sun was yellow, but not summer's sizzling yellow. It was pale. It was a winter sun.

This was the best possible time for a first day at the beach. Winter keeps most people away. Everything seems too cool—the wind, the water, and the sun. Dogs don't mind those things. They wear furry swimsuits all year round.

Miss started digging first. Match followed. When they stopped, both had damp, sandy spots on their noses. Sand as fine as sugar clung to their fur. The dogs shook hard. Ribbons of sand flew around them.

It was hard to convince the dogs to go near the water. There was too much to smell on the beach. The tide had left slippery chains of brown seaweed behind. There were also too many seashells to count. The waves had pounded them into little bits. Pink, white, and yellow scraps littered the beach for miles.

Match finally jumped in the water, but she didn't mean to do it. A clever bird tricked her.

When the dogs ran too close, the seagulls screamed and flew away. The pelicans paid no attention to the noise. They floated peacefully far from the beach. But the sandpipers were different.

The piper that taught Match to swim was smart. It ran up and down the beach like a wind-up toy with a tight spring. Match chased it back and forth. The first time Match got too close, the bird turned quickly. It opened its wings and flew swiftly over the water. Match thought the bird was playing a game, so she followed. Match didn't know that she couldn't run on water.

Suddenly, there was nothing to hold Match up. She started pumping her legs and splashing water. She came back to the beach a lot faster than she left it. The piper returned to the beach, too, flying over Match's head. Match didn't seem to notice.

Match shook hard. Her woolly fur sprayed millions of glittering water drops. She was damp but not discouraged. Her curiosity took her to a new adventure, a blue crab digging a hole in the sand. Match had something more to learn about life at the beach.

Respond to the Practice Paper

Write your answers to the following questions or directions.

1. What does the writer describe?

   _____

   _____

2. What is the first thing the puppies do after they get out of the car?

   _____

   _____

3. How does a bird trick Match into swimming?

   _____

   _____

4. Write a paragraph to summarize this description. Use these questions to help you write your summary:
   - What are the main ideas of this story?
   - What happens first? Second? Third?
   - How does the story end?

   _____

   _____

   _____

   _____

   _____

   _____

Analyze the Practice Paper

Read "First Day at the Beach" again. As you read, think about why the writer wrote this story. Write your answers to the following questions.

1. How does the writer describe the beach?

   _____

   _____

2. What descriptive words does the writer use to describe the sand?

   _____

   _____

3. Read the seventh paragraph again. Why do you think the writer wrote this paragraph?

   _____

   _____

4. How does the writer describe how the sandpiper runs?

   _____

   _____

5. Why do you think the writer describes the blue crab as a new adventure?

   _____

   _____

Writing Assignment

To describe something or someone, a writer tells what he or she sees, hears, feels, tastes, and smells. The writer also compares things, like a bird to a wind-up toy or a blue crab to an adventure. Think about an experience you would like to describe. Pay special attention to the words and comparisons you choose. Use this writing plan to help you write a first draft on the next page.

What experience would you like to describe? Write the experience in the circle. Write words and comparisons that describe the experience on the lines.

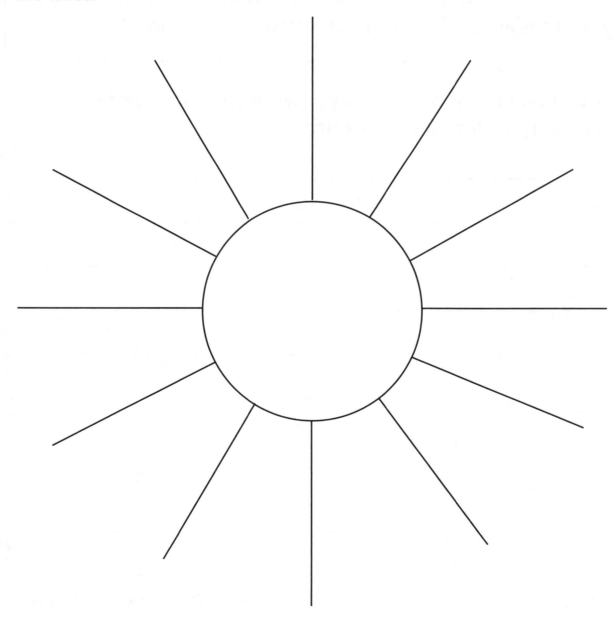

First Draft

TIPS FOR WRITING A DESCRIPTIVE STORY:

- Use your voice when you write. That means you should use your special way of expressing yourself.

- Help your reader see, smell, taste, feel, and hear what you are writing about.

- Use comparisons, or similes and metaphors, to help your readers understand what you are writing about.

Use your writing plan as a guide as you write your first draft of a descriptive story. Include a catchy title.

_____

_____

_____

_____

_____

_____

_____

(Continue on your own paper.)

Revise the Draft

Use the chart below to help you revise your draft. Check YES or NO to answer each question in the chart. If you answer NO, make notes to remind yourself how you can revise, or change, your writing to improve it.

Question	YES ✔	NO ✔	If the answer is NO, what will you do to improve your writing?
Does your story describe a specific experience?			
Do you write using your voice, or special way of expressing yourself?			
Do you use descriptive language, or words that will help your reader see, hear, taste, feel, and smell?			
Do you organize the main ideas of your story into paragraphs?			
Do you use important details to support each main idea?			
Does your story have a beginning, middle, and end?			
Have you corrected mistakes in spelling, grammar, and punctuation?			

Use the notes in your chart and your writing plan to revise your draft.

Writing Report Card

Read your revised draft again or ask someone else to read it. Have the person who reads your paper complete the following Report Card. Revise your paper until you have no less than a Very Good Score for each item.

Title of paper: _____

Purpose of paper: _*This paper is a descriptive story.*_____

Person who scores the paper: _____

Score	Writing Goals
	Does the story describe a specific experience?
	Does the descriptive story have a strong beginning, or introduction?
	Are main ideas in the descriptive story described in the order they happened?
	Are there enough details to support each main idea?
	Is the language descriptive?
	Is there a strong ending, or conclusion?
	Does the story stick to the topic?

☺ Excellent Score　　☆ Very Good Score　　+ Good Score
✔ Acceptable Score　　− Needs Improvement

UNIT 6: Short Report

HOW MUCH DO YOU KNOW?

Read the paragraph below
from a short report. Then
answer the questions.

    Where does a fish sleep? Animals
sleep in a variety of places. Raccoon cubs
curl into a ball and sleep cozily in their
den. Sea lions float in the water and sleep
at the same time. Sea otters anchor themselves to seaweed and float on
their backs. A leopard sprawls along a limb and relaxes in a tree.

1. How does the writer make you want to continue reading?

   _____

   _____

2. What is the topic sentence?

   _____

   _____

3. Which of these facts does not support the topic sentence?

   a. A leopard sprawls along a limb and relaxes in a tree.

   b. A raccoon mother stays close by her cubs while they sleep.

   c. Sea lion pups are friendly, cute, and playful.

   d. A swan can sleep while it is floating on a lake.

Analyzing a Short Report

A short report gives facts that the writer learned
by studying or by talking to experts.

Read the paragraphs below from a short
report. Then answer the questions.

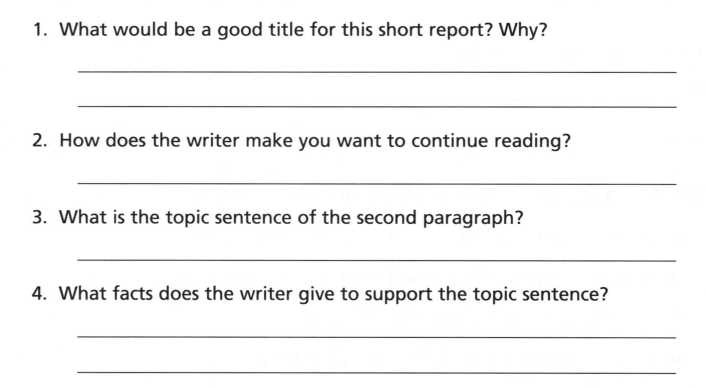

Have you ever heard a dog sing? They may
not actually sing, but dogs, wolves, and coyotes
do make a kind of music. They howl. Why do
they do it?

Scientists have several different ideas about
why these members of the dog family howl.
They believe that howling is a way for the
animals to communicate. Some scientists think that wolves may howl to call
back members of the pack that have wandered away.

1. What would be a good title for this short report? Why?

    _____

    _____

2. How does the writer make you want to continue reading?

    _____

3. What is the topic sentence of the second paragraph?

    _____

4. What facts does the writer give to support the topic sentence?

    _____

    _____

Classifying Information into Categories

> **IN A RESEARCH REPORT, GOOD WRITERS**
> - limit a topic to one category
> - group details into smaller categories

A. Imagine that you are going to write a report about animals. Write each of the words below in the three possible categories listed below them that you may use for your report. Use another piece of paper to make your chart.

polar bear	cow	boa constrictor
dog	arctic fox	walrus
jaguar	sheep	tiger
leopard	goat	reindeer
horse	bearded seal	spider monkey

1. JUNGLE ANIMALS　　2. ANIMALS OF THE ARCTIC　　3. DOMESTIC ANIMALS

B. Identify the category that was used to group each set of items below. Write the name of the category on the line.

4. _____　5. _____　6. _____

sandwich	crabs	truck
apple	sharks	skateboard
carrot stick	sunken ships	wagon
milk	coral	bicycle

Capturing the Reader's Interest

> **GOOD WRITERS**
> - create openings that capture the reader's attention
> - use closings that end what they have written in an interesting way

A. Read the following report openings and answer the questions.

a. Purple urchins are sea animals with stiff spines.

b. What lives in the ocean and looks like a pin cushion? It's a truly amazing sea animal.

1. Which opening is better? _____

2. Why is it a good opening? _____

B. For each of the following sets of facts, write an opening and a closing for a short report.

Moray eels are fish with long bodies. They live in coral reefs. During the day, they hide. At night, they hunt for crabs and other food. Moray eels have sharp teeth and look fierce. Actually, they are quite shy.

3. Opening:

_____

_____

4. Closing:

_____

_____

The octopus lives on the ocean floor. It has eight long arms and uses them to pull itself along from place to place. When an octopus is threatened by an enemy, it squirts an inky liquid into the water. The enemy may attack the ink while the octopus escapes.

5. Opening:

_____

_____

6. Closing:

_____

_____

Combining Two Sentences

> **GOOD WRITERS JOIN**
> - two short, choppy sentences into one long sentence
> - two sentences with a comma and the word *and*, *or*, or *but*

Join each pair of sentences and write the new sentence.

1. Many kinds of spiders spin webs. Not all of the webs are alike.

   _____

   _____

2. A web may be long and narrow. It may be shaped like a triangle.

   _____

   _____

3. Some webs are like funnels. Others look more like domes.

   _____

   _____

4. Wolf spiders hide in burrows. Lynx spiders live on trees or bushes.

   _____

   _____

5. Many lynx spiders are green. They are hard to find on green leaves.

   _____

   _____

6. Tarantulas are furry. They look fierce.

   _____

   _____

Proofreading a Short Report

Proofread the paragraphs from a short report, paying special attention to commas in compound sentences. Use the Proofreading Marks to correct at least seven errors.

PROOFREADING MARKS	
◯	spell correctly
⊙	add period
⋏	add comma
?	add question mark
≡	capitalize
/	make lowercase
℘	take out
⋀	add
∿	switch
¶	indent paragraph
⋁ ⋁	add quotation marks

Mountain gorillas live in the mountain

forests of Africa, usually in groups of about

ten. At night the gorillas sleep in trees or

on the ground and during the day they

look for food. They most often eat roots

and tree bark but sometimes they find

other plants to eat too. Mountain gorillas are shy animals and they are

almost always gentle. A group of gorillas may accept a scientist and the scientist might live among them for a while

Mountain gorillas communicate with each other by making sounds.

They make barking sounds when they are frightened and gorilla babies

sometimes cry. During times of danger, the group leader may roar noisily.

this noise often warns enemys away. Happy gorillas may make deep,

rumbling noises when they are eating and they make similar sounds when

they are resting.

Write an Opening and a Closing

Read an encyclopedia article or another article about a sea creature. Then write an opening and a closing for a short report about the animal. Be sure your opening captures the reader's attention. Use a closing that ends in an interesting way.

_____

_____

_____

_____

_____

_____

_____

_____

_____

_____

_____

Make a Wildlife Guide

Find out about some animals and birds that live in your state. Have each of your friends choose one animal or bird and write a short report on it. Everyone in the group can bind their reports into a booklet that you can share with family and other friends.

A Practice Short Report

THE LOST CITY

The Lost City probably isn't the kind of city you think it is. It isn't lost, either. In fact, it is a busy community sitting near the top of a mountain. The mountain is in the Atlantic Ocean. At one time, it may have been above water. But today, 700 meters (about 2,300 feet) of water cover its top.

The Lost City is a city of mounds, towers, and chimneys. The tallest chimney in the city is 18 stories. The other chimneys are smaller, but they are all made from the same materials. They are made of minerals, such as iron, copper, and sulfur. And there is life in and around these chimneys. Tiny organisms called microbes live there.

Underwater cities like the Lost City are called vent communities. The word *vent* means "opening." Scientists find most vent communities along mid-ocean ridges. Earth's crust is made of plates. Ridges form where these plates spread, or pull apart. As plates spread, ocean water sinks through cracks in the crust. The water moves downward. At the same time, lava, or melted rock, from beneath the crust moves up. It spills out through vents and heats the ocean water. The water picks up minerals from the lava. Eventually, the minerals settle, or drop out of the water. In time, they build odd and sometimes huge shapes.

Very hot water moves through chimneys on its way back to the ocean. Along the way, it meets cooler ocean water. Underwater clouds form where the hot and the cool water meet. These clouds, called smokers, are white or black. Their color depends on the kinds of minerals they hold and their temperature. White smokers are cooler and contain zinc. Black smokers are hotter and contain copper.

Many kinds of animals live near vents. They include large clams, fish, crabs, and worms. The worms are unusual. They make coverings called tubes that protect their bodies. The tubes also give them their name—tubeworms. Some tubeworms grow to be 3 meters (10 feet) long.

Scientists found the first vent community in 1977. At the time, no one knew that communities could survive without energy from the sun. On land, for example, food chains start with the sun. Plants use energy from the sun to make food. Animals get their energy from eating plants. Or they may eat animals. But sunlight doesn't reach the ocean floor. So scientists were surprised to learn that some microbes get their energy from chemicals in the water. These microbes are then food for other living things.

The Lost City is different from other vent communities. First, it is on a mountain, not on the ocean floor. Second, it doesn't have the same kinds of life.

The life around the shapes in the Lost City is different. Microbes live at the vents. But scientists think the crabs and other animals are only visiting. They continue to study life in the Lost City. One day their work may help us understand more about life in unusual places.

Respond to the Practice Paper

Write your answers to the following questions or directions.

1. What is the Lost City?

   _____

   _____

2. How did the Lost City form?

   _____

   _____

3. How are white and black smokers alike?

   _____

   _____

4. How are white and black smokers different?

   _____

   _____

5. How did the tubeworm get its name?

   _____

   _____

6. Write a paragraph to summarize the report.

   _____

   _____

   _____

   _____

Analyze the Practice Paper

Read "The Lost City" again. As you read, think about the main ideas. Pay attention to the details the writer uses to support those main ideas. Write your answers to the following questions or directions.

1. Why do you think the writer introduces the Lost City in the first sentence?

   _____

   _____

2. In the second paragraph, the writer explains what the Lost City looks like and what lives there. Name three other main ideas the writer talks about.

   _____

   _____

3. The writer uses special words, such as *microbes*, *ridges*, and *vents*. How does the writer make it easier for the reader to understand these words?

   _____

   _____

4. Why does the writer include numbers and dates in this report?

   _____

   _____

5. How are the first and last paragraphs alike?

   _____

   _____

   _____

   _____

Writing Assignment

In a short report, writers write about one topic, or subject. They research the topic to find important main ideas. They also find important details that support each main idea. Think about writing a short report about a place you would like to visit. Use this writing plan to help you write a first draft on the next page.

The topic of this paper is:

_____

Main Idea of Paragraph 1: _____

Detail: _____

Detail: _____

Detail: _____

Main Idea of Paragraph 2: _____

Detail: _____

Detail: _____

Detail: _____

Main Idea of Paragraph 3: _____

Detail: _____

Detail: _____

Detail: _____

First Draft

TIPS FOR WRITING A SHORT REPORT:

- Use reference materials to collect information about your subject.

- Take notes about important main ideas.

- Take notes about important details that support each main idea. Introduce the topic, or subject, of your report in the first paragraph.

- Organize the main ideas into separate paragraphs.

- Organize paragraphs in a logical order.

- Summarize your report in the last paragraph.

Use your writing plan as a guide as you write your first draft of a short report. Include a catchy title.

_____

_____

_____

_____

_____

_____

_____

_____

_____

(Continue on your own paper.)

Revise the Draft

Use the chart below to help you revise your draft. Check YES or NO to answer each question in the chart. If you answer NO, make notes to remind yourself how you can revise, or change, your writing to improve it.

Question	YES ✔	NO ✔	If the answer is NO, what will you do to improve your writing?
Do you write about one place in your report?			
Do you introduce the subject of your report in the first paragraph?			
Do you have more than one main idea?			
Do you organize your main ideas into paragraphs?			
Do you support each main idea with important details?			
Do you summarize your report in the last paragraph?			
Have you corrected mistakes in spelling, grammar, and punctuation?			

Use the notes in your chart and your writing plan to revise your draft.

Writing Report Card

Read your revised draft again or ask someone else to read it. Have the person who reads your paper complete the following Report Card. Revise your paper until you have no less than a Very Good Score for each item.

Title of paper: _____

Purpose of paper: _*This paper is a short report.*_____

Person who scores the paper: _____

Score	Writing Goals
	Is this writing an example of a short report?
	Does the report tell about a specific topic, or subject?
	Does the report introduce the topic in the first paragraph?
	Does the report have more than one main idea?
	Are the main ideas organized into paragraphs?
	Does the way the paragraphs are organized make sense?
	Are there details that support each main idea?
	Does the writer summarize the report in the last paragraph?
	Does the writer stick to the topic throughout the report?
	Are the report's grammar, spelling, and punctuation correct?

☺ Excellent Score   ☆ Very Good Score   + Good Score
✔ Acceptable Score   − Needs Improvement

Answer Key

Answers to the practice paper exercises questions may vary, but examples are provided here to give you an idea of how your child may respond.

Unit 1: Personal Narrative

p. 6
Possible responses:
1. He is seventy-five. He was a schoolteacher. He is married. He built a patio. 2. They were schoolteachers for 40 years. 3. They found bricks made by Grandpa Weaver.

p. 7–8
Possible responses:
1. She doesn't care much about bikes. 2. He wants his daughter to like bikes. He likes to make his daughter happy. 3. The writer discovers that her father has bought her the bike after all as a surprise. 4. They love each other.

p. 9–10
1. Cristina's shining eyes and trembling fingers, Grandma's smile, Cristina's opening her gifts and hugging the kitten, the tiny black kitten 2. Grandma's and Cristina's words, the scratching noises from the box 3. His happiness at seeing how happy he had made his sister

p. 11
Responses will vary. Be sure that each sentence includes a vivid word.

p. 12
Be sure that words are appropriate synonyms. Possible responses: 1. actually 2. unusual 3. difficult 4. glad 5, 6, 7. Responses will vary. Be sure each sentence uses an antonym.

p. 13–14
forget
Who could ever (fourget) the terrible sandstorm we had last march? It was one of
frightening
the most (frighetning) experiences of my life!

For many months there had been almost
January
no rain. December, (Janurary,) and February had been especially dry. No rain fell in March, either, but the wind began to blow furiously. On many days the sky was more
blue
brown than (blew) because the air was so filled with sand. The sand even crept inside our house. Every morning my bed felt gritty. As I walked to and from school, blowing sand stung my ears, eyes, and cheeks⊙

especially
One afternoon was (expecially) scary. We all looked anxiously through the classroom windows as the sky grew darker and darker. Our teacher, Mrs. Robertson,
story
tried to tell us a (storry,) but no one could listen. The wind howled, and we felt sand settle on our desks. Suddenly, everything
midnight
was as dark as (midnite.) The electricity had gone off!

p. 21
1. The writer wrote "A Friend at the Right Time" to explain how she met her best friend. Sunny tells us at the very beginning that this is a story that she loves to tell. 2. This story takes place at the annual school fair. 3. Although Sunny says kids drive her crazy, she takes good care of them. For instance, she saves a child when he falls from the pony. (Look for a clear understanding of Sunny's character in your child's answers. Be sure your child includes details from the narrative to support his or her understanding.) 4. Summaries will vary. Be sure your child correctly summarizes the significant events of the story, paraphrasing as needed. Summaries should be organized in a thoughtful way, with the main ideas and important details clearly presented.

p. 22
1. Sunny uses words like *I, me,* and *my* to show that she is writing about her own personal experiences. 2. A little boy is falling off the pony. Sunny has to catch the boy before he gets hurt. 3. Tiger, a very fast dog, actually solved Sunny's problem. He ran into the pony ring and led the pony out of the way so Sunny could catch the little boy. 4. A conclusion brings the story to an end. It ties up all the loose ends. 5. In the first paragraph, Sunny tells us that this story is about how she met her best friend, Tiger. The last paragraph describes exactly what Tiger did at the school fair and how Tiger became Sunny's best friend.

Unit 2: How-to Writing

p. 27
Homemade peanut butter is easy to make. First, shell the peanuts. Next, put peanuts in a blender. Blend them until they are smooth. Last, stir in a little cooking oil and salt. Spread on bread or crackers and eat!

1. Homemade peanut butter is easy to make. 2. Instructions for eating

p. 28–29
1. "Musical Chairs" is a good game to play with a group of friends. 2. It names the game. 3. It names the materials needed to play the game. 4. They tell how to play the game. 5. It tells how to decide who wins.

p. 30
Responses will vary. Be sure each answer lists the steps in correct order.
trace the outline of the kite onto a sheet of plastic; cut out the kite; glue the frame to the back of the kite; add a tail and decorations; attach the kite string

p. 31
Possible response:
Here's how to play Pin the Nose on the Clown. Draw a large clown face, but do not draw the nose. Give each player a pin and a small paper circle for the nose. Hang the clown face on a wall. Cover the first player's eyes with a cloth. The player tries to pin the nose on the clown. Keep playing until every player has had a turn. The winner is the one who pins the nose closest to the place where it belongs.

p. 32
1. Rey-Ling, Karen, and Mitch gave a party. 2. They met on Monday and Tuesday to plan the party. 3. They invited Tina, Mark, and Lee. 4. Each guest received a paper hat, a balloon, and a new pencil. 5. The children played Simon Says, Musical Chairs, and Pin the Nose on the Clown. 6. Mitch and Rey-Ling taught the others a new game. 7. Tina, Lee, and Karen sang a funny song.

p. 33–34
Do you enjoy collecting large or unusually pretty leaves? then you should learn to make ink prints of leaves. Making the prints is fun, and you'll enjoy having pretty prints of your best leaves⊙

The most important thing for making a leaf print is a leaf that you like. You also need a
larger
piece of felt just a little (lareger) than your leaf, a smooth board, a few thick sheets of plain paper, and some ink.

To begin making your leaf print, place the

felt on the board⊙ Carefully pour the ink

onto the felt until the (hole) *whole* piece is damp.

With the vein-side down, place your leaf on

the felt. Cover it with a sheet of paper, and

press down on the leaf. then take away the
            ≡

sheet of paper, pick the leaf up, and put it

ink-side down on a clean piece of paper.

Cover the leaf with another piece of paper,

and press down again⊙ When you take

away the top paper and the leaf, you'll have

your own special leaf print.

p. 41
1. This how-to paper teaches how to make a papier-mâché zoo. 2. The materials needed to make a papier-mâché zoo include old newspapers, a bucket, glue, water, paper cups, pipe cleaners, tempera paint, and paintbrushes. 3. The first step is to make papier-mâché pulp. 4. If the papier-mâché pulp is runny, it is too hard to shape. (Help your child to recognize this answer as an important detail. Discuss the importance of details such as this in a how-to paper.) 5. Answers will vary, but look for indications of understanding, such as a clear description of an animal and a corresponding illustration.

p. 42
1. The writer states the purpose of the paper clearly, lists materials, and gives clear, step-by-step instructions and helpful hints and details. 2. The writer says to collect materials before beginning the project. 3. The writer lists the materials so they can be collected before you start the project. That way, the project can be completed without wasting time finding materials. Plus, some parts of the papier-mâché process need quick action. For example, the newspapers should be torn into strips before the paste is made so the paste doesn't harden. 4. Sequence words help the reader understand the order of the steps.
5. Pictures and answers may vary. Check pictures to determine if your child understood the explanation in the sixth paragraph.

Unit 3: Fable

p. 47
1. Dove's bedroom 2. Be proud of yourself, but do not be more proud than you should be. 3. b

p. 48–49
1. the outback of Australia 2. Emu and Bowerbird 3. Emu wishes he could fly, and Bowerbird wishes he could run. 4. Emu

teaches Bowerbird to run, and Bowerbird teaches Emu to fly. 5. With a little help from a friend, you can do anything. 6. Responses will vary.

p. 50
1. c 2. Possible response: Mrs. Mason's son told her the letter was on its way. 3. no 4. yes 5. no 6. yes 7. no 8. yes 9. yes

p. 51
A. 1. She is a friendly person. 2. She sits down beside the new girl and smiles. 3. Introducing herself and inviting the new girl to play shows that she is friendly. B. Responses will vary. Be sure your child uses dialogue.

p. 52
Possible response:
Dove was dressing for Wren's party. How proud she was of her snowy white dress! It might be the most beautiful outfit at the party. Dove turned around and around. She admired her reflection in the mirror. "How lovely I look!" she cried. Then her wing bumped a bottle of ink that was sitting on her desk. The bottle turned over, and splash! Down the front of Dove's dress went an inky black stain. Moral: Be proud of yourself, but not more proud than you should be.

p. 53–54
Baby Chick peered through the tall grass

at the edge of the pond. His (freinds) *friends* Little

Duck and Little Swan splashed happily in

the water.

ˇ Come on in, Baby Chick" called Little

Duck.

"Yes," added Little Swan.ˇ The water's

nice and warm today."

Little Duck quacked ʌ "Watch me do a

trick!" Then he put his head under the water

and turned a somersault⊙

Baby Chick sighed. "I wish I could do that ʌ

he answered. "Swimming looks like such fun.

Look at my feet, though. Yours are webbed,

but mine just have little chicken toes⊙ˇ

"Don't worry," laughed Little Swan. "I'm

sure you can learn to swim anyway. Look at

this!" He proudly traced a figure (ate) *eight* in the

water.

p. 61
1. Aesop tells this story to teach us that if we are kind to others, they will be kind to us. Dove helped Ant Two. In return, Ant and Ant Two saved Dove's life. 2. Ant, Ant Two, and Dove talk, think, and have feelings, as people do. For example, Ant and Ant Two

grow tired and become cranky. They get scared, help each other, and have friendships, as people do. 3. In the beginning of the story, the setting is a big, dusty field. It is the end of summer and hot. In the middle of the story, the setting changes to a beautiful river that is surrounded by trees. The tall trees look like guards around the river. 4. Be sure your child correctly summarizes the significant events of the story, paraphrasing as needed. Summaries should be organized in a thoughtful way, with the main ideas and important details clearly presented.

p. 62
1. Aesop uses talking animals to tell the story. The ants say funny things like, "Imagine that big ball of gas (the Sun) rolling seeds across this field." The animal characters have exciting adventures like tumbling into the river. 2. Aesop shows them making jokes, feeling tired, feeling thirsty, and being scared. He shows them doing brave things and making friends. 3. Ant Two falls into the river. The human tries to catch Dove with a net. 4. Dove drops a leaf into the river and saves Ant Two. Ant and Ant Two sting the human on the legs so Dove can fly to safety. 5. Dialogue adds interest and fun to the story. The ants' conversation helps move the story along. It also shows the characters' feelings and thoughts.

Unit 4: Comparative Writing

p. 67
Comparison: 3, 5
Contrast: 1, 2, 4
6. both 7. while, instead of, unlike

p. 68–69
Comparison: 1, 2, 5
Contrast: 3, 4, 6
7. both, like, same 8. but, unlike, instead

p. 70–71
Wording may vary.
Colonial Williamsburg: Life in the 1700s. City life. Capitol, Governor's Palace, elegant houses. Both Places: Show what life was like in the past. Many shops and buildings open to tourists. Popular demonstrations of crafts. Old Sturbridge Village: Life in 1830 in a New England village. Country life. Farm, sawmill, mill for grinding grain.

p. 72
Possible responses:
1. The Hermitage is a very large house. 2. It was Andrew Jackson's home for 26 years. 3. Jackson's wife approved the site for the house. 4. Jackson had not yet been elected president when he built the house in 1819. 5. The view from the house is breathtaking. 6. Beautiful green hills can be seen from there. 7. A major fire almost destroyed the house in 1834. 8. Jackson wasted no time in rebuilding. 9. He gave many parties and invited many people.

p. 73–74
Be sure responses are appropriate

synonyms. Possible responses:
1. peaceful 2. towering, glistening
3. colorful 4. gentle 5. precious, lovely
6. fabulous 7. bustling 8. ear-splitting, frantic
9. longed-for 10. silent

p. 75–76

Texas and New mexico are neighboring
[_m̲e̲xico underlined_] *ways*
states, and in many (weighs) they are

alike. Of course, they share a common

border. Both states have large areas of land

that are dry and flat, and both states have

mountains. New Mexico's capital, santa fe,
[s̲anta f̲e underlined]
is not the state's largest city, and Austin, the

capital of Texas, is much smaller than

Houston, dallas, or San Antonio.
[d̲allas underlined]

Although new Mexico and Texas have much
[n̲ew underlined]
in common, they are different in many ways.

Some American Indians live in texas, but they
[t̲exas underlined]
make up a much larger portion of the

population of New Mexico. The land is also

different. Unlike Texas, New mexico has areas
[m̲exico underlined]
of true desert. Also, the rocky Mountains slice
[r̲ocky underlined]
through central New Mexico, giving the State
[S/state]
large areas of green forests. The mountains of

texas, in the area called Big Bend, are much
[t̲exas underlined]
drier and are not forested.

p. 82
1. This paper compares and contrasts the
American Alligator and the American
Crocodile. 2. Guide your child in organizing
the information in a clear manner.
<u>How Alligators and Crocodiles Are Alike</u>:
Both have long bodies, sharp teeth, and
tough skin.; Both are more than 15 feet long
and weigh about 450–500 pounds.; Both live
in and near freshwater and where fresh and
saltwater meet.; They drown the animals
they eat.; Both build nests to lay eggs.
<u>How Alligators and Crocodiles Are Different</u>:
An adult alligator is nearly black in color and
has a wide, flat snout. An adult crocodile is
olive-brown and has a long, narrow nose.;
Only the upper teeth are visible when an
alligator's mouth is closed, but you can see
teeth in both the upper and lower jaws when
a crocodile closes its mouth.; Alligators eat
many different kinds of food, including fish,
frogs, turtles, snakes, birds, deer, and other
alligators. Crocodiles generally eat fish,
although they may attack and eat other
animals if they come too close.; Alligators

break their prey into bite-sized pieces.
Crocodiles swallow theirs whole.; Alligator
mothers build mounds to use as nests. They
lay about 30 eggs, which hatch in about two
months. Some baby alligators stay near
their mothers for more than two years.
Female crocodiles build their nests by
digging holes in the sand or mud. They lay
about 30 to 60 eggs, which hatch about
three months later. Baby crocodiles leave
the nest a few days after birth.

p. 83
1. Talking about action movies in the first
paragraph grabs the reader's attention.
2. The writer says, "But there's more to
these reptiles than you think." Then the
writer invites you to take a closer look.
3. The writer uses the sixth paragraph to
change the main idea. The writer says,
"Now let's talk about what they eat and
where they lay their eggs." 4. The seventh
paragraph describes what alligators eat. The
eighth paragraph tells what crocodiles eat.
Talking about alligators and then crocodiles
makes it easier for the reader to understand
how the animals are alike and different. 5. In
the introduction, the writer talks about
animals in the movies. By writing about the
movies again in the conclusion, the writer
finishes the idea and relates the first and
last paragraphs.

Unit 5: Descriptive Writing

p. 89
1. Yellowstone National Park has some of
the strangest scenery. 2. The smell of pine
trees fills the air. 3. b, d

p. 90
1. The wintry scene looked like an artist's
dream. 2. It suggests what the paragraph is
about and sets the mood. 3. The clip-
clopping of the horses; their jingling harness
bells 4. The passengers breathing icy air
and snuggling into blankets; the cold of the
stone towers 5. Rows of towering pines,
their branches drooping with snow; the
castle poking its towers into the gray sky;
bright red and purple blankets 6. The writer
begins by telling about things on the ground
and moves up, ending in the sky.

p. 91–92
Wording may vary slightly.
shadows; broken windows; overgrown with
weeds; crows circling; Drooping branches; a
dark cloud; cold, damp air; old, musty smell;
cobwebs; creaking door.

p. 93
1. the lake, a golden mirror 2. mountain
peaks, jagged teeth 3. the setting sun, a
melting ball of wax; 4. the sunset, a pink
and orange flame
5, 6, 7. Responses will vary. Be sure that
similes and metaphors are descriptive.

p. 94
Be sure each answer is two sentences or a
compound sentence. Possible responses:
1. Our boat chugged into the bay. We saw

that the opposite shore was covered by
solid ice. 2. The mountain of ice was a
glacier. It rose straight up out of the water.
3. I moved out onto the deck, and an icy
wind blistered my face. 4. Our boat chugged
nearer to the wall of ice. The wind grew
even colder.
5. Now I could see jagged pieces of ice
floating in the water. Some had furry
passengers. 6. The passengers were soft-
eyed seals. They stared at me without fear.
7. We drew close to the glacier. Then we
heard a loud rumbling. 8. A chunk of ice fell
from the glacier. It dropped into the water.

p. 95–96

On this sunny day, the crowded beach is as

busy as a school playground during recess.
 s
Far from the waves, families spreads

blankets on the sand and share picnic
 s
lunches. A child dig^ in the sand while his
 ∧
older brother and sister toss a beach ball

back and forth. A little nearer the water,

huge umbrellas sprout like brightly-colored
 s
mushrooms. Men and women stretches out

in the shade to read or nap. At the edge of
 s
the ocean, a small girl build^ a sand castle.
 ∧
 s
Her brother look^ for pretty shells and helps
 ∧
her decorate the castle walls⊙ The soft

sand and shallow water attract children of all
 s
ages. They runs and splash where the
 beach
water laps the (beech). Farther from shore∧
 s
strong swimmers rides the waves. Floating
 thier
on (there) backs, they look like playful

dolphins. Out where the waves spray white

foam, a few surfboards skim across the
 s
water. The boards rises and plunge on the

waves like crazy elevators.

p. 101
1. The writer describes the first time the two
puppies, Miss and Match, go to the beach.
2. As soon as their paws touch the sand, the
puppies freeze. 3. A sandpiper runs up and
down the beach. Match chases after it.
Suddenly, the piper turns and flies out over
the water. Match, without thinking, follows.
Match runs into the water and then swims
back to the beach. 4. Be sure that your child
correctly summarizes the significant events
of the story, paraphrasing as needed. Main
ideas should be organized logically and
important details presented clearly.

p. 102

1. The writer describes the beach as always changing. The water changes from blue to gray. The sand is almost white. The sun is pale and weak. The beach is empty and cool for people but perfect for dogs. 2. The sand is white and fine as sugar. 3. The writer teases the reader with information. This makes the reader curious, so the reader keeps reading to find out what happens.
4. The writer compares the sandpiper to a wind-up toy with a tight spring. 5. The writer wants the reader to know that the dogs do more exciting things at the beach.

Unit 6: Short Report

p. 107

1. by making you wonder where animals sleep 2. Animals sleep in a variety of places. 3. c

p. 108

1. Possible response: Animals That Make Music 2. by making you wonder why animals howl 3. Scientists have several different ideas about why these members of the dog family howl. 4. They believe that howling is a way for the animals to communicate. Some scientists think that wolves may howl to call back members of the pack that have wandered away.

p. 109

Word order in each list may vary.
1. jaguar, leopard, boa constrictor, tiger, spider monkey 2. polar bear, arctic fox, bearded seal, walrus, reindeer 3. dog, horse, cow, sheep, goat
4, 5, 6. Responses will vary. Be sure each answer is a category into which all the items will fit.

p. 110–111

1. b 2. It gets the reader's attention.
3, 4, 5, 6. Responses will vary. Be sure that the opening and closing are suitable.

p. 112

Possible responses:
1. Many kinds of spiders spin webs, but not all of the webs are alike. 2. A web may be long and narrow, or it may be shaped like a triangle. 3. Some webs are like funnels, but others look more like domes. 4. Wolf spiders hide in burrows, but lynx spiders live on trees or bushes. 5. Many lynx spiders are green, and they are hard to find on green leaves.
6. Tarantulas are furry, and they look fierce.

p. 113–114

Mountain gorillas live in the mountain forests of Africa, usually in groups of about ten. At night the gorillas sleep in trees or on the ground and during the day they look for food. They most often eat roots and tree bark, but sometimes they find other plants to eat, too. Mountain gorillas are shy animals, and they are almost always gentle. A group of gorillas may accept a scientist, and the scientist might live among them for a while.

Mountain gorillas communicate with each other by making sounds. They make barking sounds when they are frightened, and gorilla babies sometimes cry. During times of danger, the group leader may roar noisily. enemies this noise often warns (enemys) away. Happy gorillas may make deep, rumbling noises when they are eating, and they make similar sounds when they are resting.

p. 119

1. The Lost City is a community located on top of a mountain under the Atlantic Ocean. 2. The Lost City formed when cool ocean water met hot lava. The water picked up minerals from the lava. Later, the minerals settled out and built strange forms like mounds, towers, and chimneys. 3. Both black and white smokers are underwater clouds that form when very hot water moves through vents and meets cooler ocean water. 4. Black smokers are hotter than white smokers. Also, black smokers contain copper, while white smokers contain zinc. 5. The worms that live near vents make coverings called tubes to protect themselves, so they are called tubeworms. 6. Be sure that your child identifies the report's main ideas and includes significant details.

p. 120

1. The first paragraph of a short report introduces the topic. Because the topic of this report has such an interesting, mysterious name, the writer includes it in the first sentence to encourage the reader to keep reading. 2. The other main ideas in this report are how vent communities form, how living things survive in vent communities, and how the Lost City is different from other vent communities. 3. The writer uses simpler words to define each word that the reader might not know. 4. The writer uses facts like numbers and dates to make the report more accurate. Facts also show the reader that the writer probably used reference materials to find information for the report. 5. The first paragraph introduces the topic of this report. The last paragraph summarizes the topic.